The Social Work Portfolio

The
Social Work
Portfolio

PLANNING, ASSESSING, AND DOCUMENTING LIFELONG LEARNING IN A DYNAMIC PROFESSION

BARRY R. COURNOYER

MARY J. STANLEY

BROOKS/COLE
CENGAGE Learning

Australia • Brazil • Japan • Korea • Mexico • Singapore • Spain • United Kingdom • United States

BROOKS/COLE
CENGAGE Learning™

The Social Work Portfolio:
Planning, Assessing, and Documenting
Lifelong Learning in a Dynamic Profession
Barry R. Cournoyer, Mary J. Stanley

Publisher: Edith Beard Brady

Sponsoring Editor: Lisa Gebo

Assistant Editor: Shelley Gesicki

Marketing: Caroline Concilla and
Megan Hansen

Production Editor: Mary Vezilich

Production Service: G&S Typesetters

Permissions Editor: Sue Ewing

Editorial Assistant: Sheila Walsh

Cover Design: Denise Davidson

Cover Illustration: Lisa Henderling/SIS

Print Buyer: Kris Waller

Typesetting: G&S Typesetters

For product information and technology assistance, contact us at
Cengage Learning Customer & Sales Support, 1-800-354-9706

For permission to use material from this text or product,
submit all requests online at **www.cengage.com/permissions**
Further permissions questions can be emailed to
permissionrequest@cengage.com

Library of Congress Control Number: 2001035977

ISBN-13: 978-0-534-34305-7

ISBN-10: 0-534-34305-8

Brooks/Cole
10 Davis Drive
Belmont, CA 94002-3098
USA

Cengage Learning is a leading provider of customized learning solutions with office locations around the globe, including Singapore, the United Kingdom, Australia, Mexico, Brazil, and Japan. Locate your local office at:
www.cengage.com/global

Cengage Learning products are represented in Canada by Nelson Education, Ltd.

To learn more about Brooks/Cole, visit **www.cengage.com/brookscole**

Purchase any of our products at your local college store or at our preferred online store
www.ichapters.com

Printed in the United States of America
9 10 11 12 12 11 10

Contents

Preface

Over the course of the past decade, we have become convinced that *learning how to learn* and *lifelong learning* are, on balance, even more important for social work students than the acquisition of professional knowledge itself. Unless social work students become active, self-directed, and collaborative learners during their B.S.W., M.S.W., or doctoral programs, they will be unlikely to engage energetically in lifelong learning opportunities following graduation. As a result, the quality and effectiveness of their service to clients will certainly diminish over time. In this era of constant change and heightened accountability, the social work portfolio represents a means to plan, assess, and document the nature, scope, and quality of learning during and following formal university study.

We designed this small book to help students prepare a social work portfolio to serve several important professional functions. First and foremost, the portfolio can promote and guide your own learning—whether that learning occurs in a formal academic setting or elsewhere. In essence, the portfolio helps you develop the attitudes, skills, and habits of active, self-directed, and collaborative lifelong learning. It is a means and context for establishing and revising personal and professional learning goals, assessing the quality and relevance of your learning, and documenting progress. Second, the portfolio is a place to store and update your professional résumé and to record those learning experiences needed to complete a course or earn a social work degree. Social work programs increasingly use student portfolios as a fundamental component of their overall approach to teaching and learning. Well-designed student portfolios can promote the development of critical thinking skills and enhance the integration of learning across curriculum areas. In some social work programs, entering students begin to prepare portfolios during their first courses. Then they extend and refine them throughout their program of studies. Students include selected products from various classroom and field practicum experiences and regularly engage in reflective self-evaluation of their professional growth and development. They periodically share evolving portfolios with their advisers and colleagues and then submit a final version for summary review as they near completion of their coursework, perhaps during a capstone course.

Following graduation, portfolios help social workers maintain their social work licenses or other pertinent professional credentials. Most certification policies and licensing laws require social workers to document completion of a minimum number of continuing education units (CEUs) each year through participation in courses, seminars, or workshops. Indeed, continuing professional learning is becoming ever more important in our efforts to provide competent, ethical, and effective social work services to an increasingly diverse client population in a constantly changing society. The knowledge explosion continues to expand at a dizzying pace.

New information emerges so rapidly that all helping professionals must be prepared to discover, analyze, and if relevant, apply innovative knowledge in their service to others. To serve clients and society competently, social workers must be enthusiastic lifelong learners—reading, observing, listening, studying, reflecting, conversing, collaborating, analyzing, synthesizing, and evaluating—during academic programs of study and continuing on throughout their professional lives. The social work portfolio contributes to your lifelong learning abilities and activities.

Third, the portfolio may be used during job placement interviews or as part of an application to various agencies or to programs of higher education. Résumés are becoming insufficient. Supplemental information is usually required. Portfolios can serve that function.

Importantly, portfolios may be used by schools and departments of social work to serve program assessment and evaluation purposes. Independent review of social work students' portfolios serves as a form of assessment of student learning. Such assessment processes reveal strengths and weaknesses in academic programming, curricula, or instructional methods. The Council on Social Work Education (CSWE) requires accredited programs to assess progress toward their goals, especially those that involve student learning. Portfolios can be an important dimension of a program's approach to assessment of the nature, depth, and scope of student learning.

We sincerely believe that if you conscientiously read this book, complete the exercises, prepare a social work portfolio during the course of your academic program, and maintain it throughout your professional career, you will be a better social worker. You will become a more energetic, self-directed, and collaborative learner who experiences lifelong learning as a natural and satisfying aspect of professional social work service.

Suggestions for Social Work Educators and Students

This book is intended primarily for use by social work students currently engaged in formal educational programs of study (e.g., B.S.W., M.S.W., D.S.W., or Ph.D.). We think maximum benefit occurs when students begin to use the book early in their professional studies (e.g., a sophomore or first semester junior in a B.S.W. program or a first semester M.S.W. or doctoral student). Then they may proceed to plan, assess, and document their learning through the use of evolving social work portfolios in all their classroom and field courses. However, students may also use the book toward the end of their academic studies, perhaps in a capstone seminar, where learning gained and documents prepared throughout their program may be reviewed, assessed, and compiled during a focused period of time.

Social work educators will, of course, have their own views of the value and utility of portfolios and may appropriately advise their students accordingly. We recommend, however, that faculty encourage the development of student portfolios that address certain dimensions. First, we suggest that the social work program's major student learning goals are clearly reflected in all portfolios. Indeed, the social work portfolio is a forum for students to demonstrate their learning in these key areas. For example, suppose a department of social work identified "competence in generalist social work practice" as a goal that all students are expected to achieve by graduation. Each portfolio, then, would contain documentary evidence (e.g., papers, field performance evaluations) to support the student's demonstration of competence in generalist practice.

Second, we urge educators to encourage students to include within their portfolios products that reflect their knowledge, attitudes, and abilities within major curriculum areas (e.g., social work values and ethics, diversity, populations at risk, social and economic justice, human behavior and the social environment, social welfare policy and services, social work practice, research, and the field practicum).

Third, we encourage faculty to advise students to use their portfolios to demonstrate growth in professional knowledge, values, and expertise over time. In other words, products prepared during the final semesters of coursework should be of noticeably better quality, with greater professionalism and intellectual sophistication than those submitted in the first or second semester. Student portfolios should contain evidence that reflects professional development (i.e., learning) over the course of the academic program.

Fourth, we suggest that faculty expect students to include within their portfolios evidence of developing self-awareness, self-assessment, scholarship, and critical thinking along with a capacity and commitment to engage in active, self-directed learning.

Finally, educators should carefully review and assess the social work portfolios prepared by students. Each student should receive thorough evaluative feedback concerning the contents and quality of the portfolio. If students' portfolios are viewed as unimportant paperwork, if they are ignored, or if they are reviewed casually, their value and utility will quickly decrease. Educators charged with the responsibility of assessing and evaluating portfolios and those who compile and report aggregated results should receive significant credit for such important duties. And copies of some (i.e., a random sample of adequate size) or all student portfolios should be stored so that cohort comparisons may be made over time. Educators might reasonably predict that the average quality of the portfolios and the evidence of improved student learning reflected by them will increase with each passing year.

Social work students are also likely to have various views of the utility of student portfolios. Some may perceive them as a form of additional busywork, especially if faculty and program administrators consider them of limited value. Others may recognize the value of portfolios for themselves and their own professional growth. Indeed, we encourage all students to consider the potential benefits of preparing a social work portfolio and developing independent and collaborative learning skills during their formal educational studies. Importantly, the social work portfolio may become a means to organize, integrate, and focus lifelong learning activities of all kinds.

Structure of the Book

We have organized the book as follows: In Chapter 1, we introduce you to the social work portfolio and explore its relationship to learning. We also present an overview of the contemporary context of practice and highlight the importance of active, self-directed, and collaborative lifelong learning in the dynamic social work profession. We discuss both independent and group forms of learning and encourage you to begin the process of self-directed lifelong learning. In Chapter 2, we help you explore your learning self, including your multiple intelligences, emotional intelligence, psychological type, and your personal learning style. The exercises provide you with opportunities to discover aspects of yourself that may affect how you learn and what you might do to enhance your learning skills and abilities.

In Chapter 3, we engage you in a process of self-assessment to help you determine your social work learning needs. We help you explore your current level of knowledge and expertise in those content areas most relevant for social workers today. In Chapter 4, we help you organize and assess your prior learning, begin to establish a general career plan, and identify an ideal social work position. In this chapter, we ask you to collect various documents and to prepare a résumé for inclusion within your social work portfolio.

In Chapter 5, we ask you to identify specific learning goals and objectives and to prepare personal learning plans by which to pursue, assess, and document progress toward their achievement. We hope the experience serves as a model for developing additional personal learning plans for years to come. In Chapter 6, we guide you through the compilation and assessment of your social work portfolio with an emphasis on learning activities during your academic program. We conclude the book by presenting guidelines for continuing to adapt, refine, and use the social work portfolio throughout your professional career.

Throughout the book, we recognize the relevance of critical thinking, scholarship, and continuous lifelong learning for effective social work practice in contemporary society. We also emphasize the need for both independent and group learning activities and stress the importance of writing as a means to enhance critical thinking and related professional abilities. Each chapter contains independent and collaborative group exercises to help you prepare a social work portfolio and, importantly, develop abilities for lifelong learning throughout your professional career.

Acknowledgments

We would like to thank our reviewers for their helpful comments: Christine Diggs, Virginia State University; Bart Grossman, University of California, Berkeley; Marlene Huff, University of Kentucky; Betsy J. Page, Kent State University; Joan Saltman, West Virginia University; Tina Timm, Saint Louis University; and Evelyn Williams, University of North Carolina, Chapel Hill.

We dedicate this book to our loving and supportive spouses—Catherine Hughes Cournoyer and Michael Stanley; our incredibly wonderful children—John Paul and Michael Cournoyer, and Jill Lynn Pursell and Jeffrey Michael Stanley; and to Mary's grandchildren—Jessica Elaine Stanley and Brandon Alexander Stanley.

Barry R. Cournoyer
Mary J. Stanley

About the Authors

Barry R. Cournoyer has been a social worker for more than 27 years and a university professor for more than 20. He served as Associate Dean for Quality Improvement at the Indiana University School of Social Work for nearly 5 years. During his tenure as associate dean, he became interested in student learning, portfolios, and assessment of student outcomes.

At Indiana University, he teaches social work practice courses, primarily at the master's and Ph.D. levels. Author of *The Social Work Skills Workbook* (3rd ed., Brooks/Cole–Wadsworth), he remains very interested in students' development of cognitive, intrapersonal, and interpersonal skills and abilities. Along with his wife, Catherine, he also maintains a small independent practice where they provide social work services to individuals, couples, and families.

Mary J. Stanley began work in a local library at the age of 15 when she was officially hired as a library page to shelve books. She stayed with the public library system through high school, college, and graduation. She progressed from library page to clerical positions and finally to the role of children's librarian. She primarily served residents of the inner city, enabling poverty-level families and transients to use the resources of the public library system. These experiences marked the beginning of her involvement with social workers and their clients.

Approximately 20 years ago, she accepted a position at the Indiana University–Purdue University Indianapolis (IUPUI) campus library. After a few years, she assumed the role of social work reference librarian and liaison to the Indiana University School of Social Work. She maintains the social work collection for the modern, state-of-the-art, hi-tech IUPUI university library, assists social work students and faculty in research pursuits, and educates them about library resources and usage. She serves as Associate Dean of the IUPUI library and as Adjunct Associate Professor of Social Work with Indiana University.

Over the years, she has delivered numerous workshops and seminars to social work students and faculty at local, regional, and national levels. She has published papers related to social work education and has twice served as chair of the national Social Work Librarians' Interest Group.

THE SOCIAL WORK PORTFOLIO AND LIFELONG LEARNING

As a social worker in the 21st century, you will face unprecedented professional challenges. The pace of change in research and information development, already incredibly rapid, continues to increase. Keeping abreast of emerging knowledge during the "third wave" information and technology age (Toffler, 1983) represents a major test of both intellect and motivation—even if you happen to be a voracious learner. Added to the pressure of maintaining familiarity with current advances in theoretical and empirical knowledge, you also confront the dual challenges of competition and accountability. Greater competition and heightened demands for accountability are evident in all service delivery systems, all practice contexts, and all forms of social work practice. To meet these expectations, social workers must demonstrate competence and continuous growth and development as professionals. Contemporary social workers must be active, self-directed, and effective learners throughout their careers. *The Social Work Portfolio* can help you plan, assess, and document your lifelong learning activities.

In this chapter (see Box 1.1), we introduce you to the social work portfolio—a compilation of documents that you develop, use, revise, and reuse for various purposes during your academic studies and throughout your career as a practicing social worker. We also discuss the challenging context of contemporary social work and highlight the relationship of the social work portfolio to lifelong learning.

The Social Work Portfolio [1]

Portfolios are widely used in many contexts to demonstrate talents, abilities, competencies, achievements, and potential. Artists and photographers, for example, commonly maintain selections of their artistic work in portfolios. Then, when applying for a job, bidding on a contract, applying to graduate schools or institutes, and seeking to display their work in art galleries, they present examples of their artistic creations. Portfolios may be used in other contexts as well. A collection of written products, especially those that have been assessed or evaluated, along with a well-prepared résumé can reflect the depth and breadth of your learning as a social worker. The products that you complete as part of various formal and informal learning experiences may be included in your portfolio.

We view the social work portfolio as:

A well-organized and carefully prepared collection of documents related to one's readiness for professional social work practice. The portfolio reflects documentary evidence of an active, self-directed approach to learning and ongoing growth as a social work student or practitioner. Essential components include a table of contents; an introductory statement that refers to one's professional aspirations and learning goals; a

[1] Adapted from Appendix 1: The Social Work Skills Learning Portfolio in *The Social Work Skills Workbook*, Third Edition, by Barry Cournoyer. Copyright © 2000 Brooks/Cole—Wadsworth.

BOX

1.1   **CHAPTER PURPOSES**

The purposes of this chapter are to introduce you to the social work portfolio as a means to plan, assess, and document learning throughout your academic program and your professional career, to explore some of the challenges associated with modern social work, and to discuss the importance of lifelong learning for competent social work practice in the 21st century.

Goals

Following completion of this chapter, you should be able to:

- Describe a social work portfolio
- Identify the major components and some of the functions of the social work portfolio
- Discuss the challenges associated with modern social work
- Discuss the significance of those challenges for lifelong learning
- Describe how a social work portfolio contributes to lifelong learning and effective professional service

résumé; a selection of products and accompanying self-assessments that reflect the nature and quality of one's knowledge, attitudes, and expertise; a summary that highlights the most significant components of the portfolio; and appendixes that contain pertinent materials such as copies of transcripts, diplomas, certificates, awards, and letters of recognition.

Social work portfolios may be organized in several different ways. You might prepare a "book" with a table of contents, several sections or chapters, and appendixes. You could compile your documents and products within an expandable accordion-type folder. Or if you are technologically adept, you might create a social work portfolio compact disc or Web site for "point and click" access to various folders and pages. Most people prefer the convenience of preparing sections of their portfolios with the aid of a personal computer and associated word-processing software. Then they save components of their portfolio to a computer hard drive or removable storage device (e.g., floppy disk, Zip disk, or CD-ROM) for easy editing and printing. Indeed, the social work portfolio reaches its maximum potential when its components are word processed and stored in electronic form. Regardless of the particular medium you use to store the elements of your portfolio, however, you will need several folders—of the cardboard or computerized variety—to access documents quickly and efficiently.

Your social work portfolio will be unique. No one else could—or should—adopt your career aspirations, replicate your résumé, or duplicate your learning goals. Indeed, you might prepare alternative versions of your portfolio to accomplish different purposes. For instance, you might organize it in one way for a particular classroom or field course, in a second to meet the requirements for a university degree, in a third manner to enhance your prospects for employment or as part of your application to a graduate school or institute, and in yet a different form to plan, assess, and document your own professional growth and development as a practicing social worker.

Although unique and individualized, your portfolio should contain several essential sections: First, an easily updated table of contents helps guide readers to relevant sections within the portfolio. Second, an introduction provides overall context and perspective concerning the purposes of the portfolio in light of your academic or career aspirations and learning goals. Third, a résumé helps present important milestones in your personal, educational, and professional history. Fourth, various learning products (e.g., papers you have written) and corresponding self-assessments serve as documentary evidence of learning progress. Fifth, a summary section permits you to consider, analyze, and evaluate the nature, quality, and relevance of your learning in light of academic program expectations and your career directions. Sixth, appendixes that contain additional documentation (e.g., copies of degrees and certificates or licenses, academic transcripts, performance appraisals) provide further evidentiary support.

These sections constitute the primary components of the social work portfolio. Of course, you may add others to address specific purposes and functions. Consider the portfolio as an ongoing work in progress. We suggest that you begin the portfolio at the very beginning of your social work academic program and maintain it through graduation. Thereafter, you may add to, revise, and update your portfolio as you progress through your professional career.

We also recommend that you occasionally reflect upon and assess the quality of your portfolio and periodically submit it to one or more colleagues for review and feedback. At times, you will prepare a formal version that includes a selected collection of products that have been carefully revised and reworked to reflect your very best work. Formal portfolios may be required for completion of a course or academic program, or they may be expected as part of an interview process. Regardless of the particular version, however, all portfolios represent means and contexts by which to plan, assess, and document your learning.

Contemporary Social Work: Issues and Challenges

As a social worker in contemporary society, you will confront many challenges and numerous obstacles in your attempts to provide high-quality, effective services to an increasingly diverse clientele addressing a vast array of social issues. You do so in a context of greater accountability and competition than ever before. Helping professionals from various academic disciplines now compete with one another for employment and seek to expand or protect traditional service delivery territories. Both the bachelor of social work and the master of social work degrees continue to be highly valued throughout the human service field. Social work is projected to be one of the fastest growing professions well into the 21st century. Persons with social work doctorates are truly in great demand, particularly within academic and research settings. Nonetheless, along with the anticipated gain in the overall number of social workers, you may expect comparable growth within other human service professions as well. A social work education is increasingly viewed by employers as only one of several legitimate educational paths through which to prepare for human service positions. In considering whom to employ, competence and accountability are among the major factors that guide agency supervisors and administrators. As they evaluate employment applications, they consider questions such as the following:

- Who is most likely to provide high-quality, ethical, effective, and efficient services to clients?

- Who is most likely to demonstrate responsibility and accountability, maintain up-to-date records and reports, and least likely to engage in behavior that might harm clients or increase agency liability?

- Who is most up to date with recent advances and innovations, and who is most likely to keep current with emerging knowledge in the future?

- Who is most capable of thinking critically and analytically, writing clearly, and most likely to engage nondefensively in personal and professional self-reflection, self-assessment, and self-evaluation?

Social workers who reflect these qualities have a high "employability quotient" and readily secure preferred positions in modern health, mental-health, education, and human service agencies. They find themselves in great demand and often struggle to decide which of several offers to accept. They are also likely to be extremely attractive to social work graduate programs that seek to recruit students that are active, self-directed, independent, and collaborative learners who think critically and write well.

Lifelong Learning and the Information Age

To meet the increasingly rigorous expectations of modern professional social work and to serve clients well, you will need to develop and enhance your knowledge and expertise both during your academic program of study and throughout your entire career. As a contemporary social worker, you must know how to learn and then engage continuously in lifelong learning. And you must do so in the midst of the ever-expanding knowledge explosion characteristic of the information age. In an attempt to provide some context and clarity, we propose the following working definition:

> Lifelong learning for social work refers to ongoing processes associated with the acquisition or construction of information, knowledge, and understanding; the development, adoption, and reconsideration of values and attitudes; and the development of skills and expertise through coursework, experience, observation, conversation, and study from the time someone first explores social work as an educational or professional career choice to the time that person no longer considers him- or herself a social worker. Lifelong learning experiences can be formal (e.g., a college course or professional seminar) or informal (e.g., an enlightening conversation with another person or a tragic but meaningful life experience). They may be self-initiated or guided by others, independent or collaborative, and planned or unplanned.

Much of human society has entered the information and technology age. In advanced "third wave" societies (Toffler, 1983), knowledge is an extraordinarily valuable commodity—often more valuable than tangible resources such as land, stocks and bonds, factories, or even cash. A new kind of class system is emerging. "Haves" will increasingly be distinguished from "have-nots" by the ease and extent to which they access and use knowledge. In effect, the most at-risk populations will be those who cannot or do not continuously unlearn obsolete, invalid, and irrelevant information and relearn current, accurate, and pertinent knowledge and skills.

According to Davis and Botkin (1994), the total knowledge in the world, on average, doubles about every 7 years. In some subject areas, knowledge doubling occurs even more rapidly. As many of us realize from the rapid obsolescence of computer hardware and software, the rate of change in computer science is simply astonishing. The knowledge explosion, however, is not limited to high technology. The liberal arts and sciences and all the helping professions are dramatically affected as well.

We assert that some of the material that you currently study in your social work courses is already obsolete. By graduation, information you learned 1 year or 2 years previously will be outdated as well. With each passing year, more and more of what you studied in school will become less and less relevant, accurate, and useful. The life span of knowledge for social work is surprisingly short. Unless you continuously and aggressively seek additional learning following graduation, you will inexorably fall further and further behind the knowledge curve. If you fail to keep current with contemporary research findings and advances in practice expertise, your clients will probably suffer. As social workers in service to potentially vulnerable populations, you must be an incessant and voracious learner. We think that you, as a social work student, must learn *how to learn* before you graduate. In particular, we believe that you should learn how to plan, assess, and document your learning. As Eric Hoffer (1973) suggested:

> The central task of education is to implant a will and facility for learning; it should produce not learned but learning people. The truly human society is a learning society, where grandparents, parents, and children are students together.
>
> In a time of drastic change, it is the learners who inherit the future. The learned usually find themselves equipped to live in a world that no longer exists. (p. 22)

As society continues to progress from the second wave industrial to the third wave information and technology age, a related form of revolution is also underway. Spurred by changing values and a dramatically different technological environment, means and methods of teaching and learning are undergoing radical transformations. Mass education, so valuable for "second wave" industrial societies, is becoming "de-massified" (Toffler & Toffler, 1995) to address the learning needs of individuals and communities. Increasingly, professors, departments, schools, and in some instances, entire universities are shifting their emphasis from "teaching" to "learning" (Hooker, 1997; Oblinger & Rush, 1997). There is also a shift from "one size fits all" generic curricula to individualized or personal learning plans and contracts that address the unique learning needs of particular people.

In the United States, this transition is associated with the seminal work of the late Malcolm Knowles (1980, 1984, 1989, 1990, 1992). For most of the 20th century, a pedagogical paradigm dominated educational institutions throughout North America. *Pedagogy* is a term derived from the Greek words *paid* (meaning "child") and *agogus* (meaning "leading"). Thus, the word *pedagogy* literally means the art and science of leading or teaching children.

Knowles suggested that most people are natural learners, although they are often inefficient and ineffective in their approach. They want to develop abilities that will serve them throughout their personal and professional lifetimes. In particular, they seek to become effective learners able to: (a) assess their own learning needs; (b) define their own learning goals; (c) set their own learning objectives; (d) select means, approaches, and resources to achieve learning goals and objectives; (e) use both internal and external experiences and resources for the purposes of learning; and (f) incorporate lifelong learning activities within and around personal and professional activities.

Toward the latter portion of his career, Knowles placed greater emphasis upon self-directed learning. He wrote:

> On the assumption that the primary purpose of schooling is to help individuals develop the skills of learning, the ultimate behavioral objective of schooling is: *'The individual engages efficiently in collaborative self-directed inquiry in self-actualizing directions.'* I believe that these skills of learning include at least the following:
>
> 1. The ability to develop and be in touch with curiosities. Perhaps another way to describe this skill would be 'the ability to engage in divergent thinking.'
> 2. The ability to perceive one's self objectively and accept feedback about one's performance non-defensively.
> 3. The ability to diagnose one's learning needs in the light of models of competencies required for performing life roles.
> 4. The ability to formulate learning objectives in terms that describe performance outcomes.
> 5. The ability to identify human, material, and experiential resources for accomplishing various kinds of learning objectives.

6. The ability to design a plan of strategies for making use of appropriate learning resources effectively.
7. The ability to carry out a learning plan systematically and sequentially. This skill is the beginning of the ability to engage in convergent thinking.
8. The ability to collect evidence of the accomplishment of learning objectives and have it validated through performance. (Knowles, 1990, p. 174)

Malcolm Knowles's papers and books continue to generate much discussion and considerable application within academic settings. Two other publications have caused quite a stir as well. Chickering and Gamson (1987) analyzed more than 50 years of research related to the topic of effective teaching and learning. Their analysis yielded seven principles for good practice in higher education. These principles apply to professional social work education at both the baccalaureate and graduate levels. They also relate to the processes of continuing professional education and lifelong learning for social work.

As suggested by Chickering and Gamson, learning is likely to be especially effective when learners: interact frequently, form cooperative learning teams, undertake active learning experiences, give and receive prompt and constructive feedback, spend sufficient "time on task," have high expectations, and respect diverse talents and ways of learning. The beneficial effects are most powerful when they occur simultaneously in a learning context. "Together they employ six powerful forces in education: activity, expectations, cooperation, interaction, diversity, and responsibility" (Chickering & Gamson, 1987, p. 4).

Complementing Chickering and Gamson's analysis, Barr and Tagg (1995) compared aspects of the traditional "instructional paradigm" with an emerging "learning paradigm." They suggested that institutions of higher education have tended to focus more on the teacher and the instruction than on the student and the learning. According to Barr and Tagg, the major purpose of the traditional instructional paradigm is to transfer knowledge from teachers to students. Conversely, the primary purpose of the learning paradigm is to encourage student discovery and construction of knowledge. Under the learning paradigm, knowledge is shaped and constructed by the learners themselves. All students are viewed as talented, capable learners—albeit sometimes in different ways and at different speeds.

In the new learning paradigm, learners: (a) assume individual and collective responsibility for learning; (b) cooperate with one another; (c) actively seek, discover, and construct information; and (d) use and apply information to understand, assess, analyze, and address real problems.

Principles for Lifelong Learning in Social Work

In this chapter, we have introduced you to the social work portfolio and discussed the nature and importance of lifelong learning for effective professional practice during the knowledge explosion so characteristic of the information and technology age. However, we have yet to discuss values or principles that might guide your learning activities and the development and assessment of your social work portfolio. Most social workers are well acquainted with the core social work values and professional ethics that serve us well in our efforts to help others. Indeed, some of them relate directly to learning. However, others do not. Therefore, we would like to propose a set of principles to guide you as you plan, assess, and document your learning and prepare your portfolio.

We derive these principles primarily from the work of Linda Elder and Richard Paul of the Center for Critical Thinking (2000; Foundation for Critical Thinking, 2000; Paul, 1993). They propose several "universal intellectual standards" and "valuable intellectual traits" that serve as an excellent basis for the development of essential value-based guidelines for lifelong learning in social work. These principles include: humility; empathy; fairness; courage; honesty and integrity; clarity, precision, and accuracy; relevance; intellectual sophistication; and logic. We have adapted them for social workers engaged in learning of all kinds (e.g., in a formal academic course or program, while staffing a case with professional colleagues, during a professional conference or workshop, or throughout the process of serving clients).

Humility Social workers reflect the value of humility in learning when we are keenly aware of the limits of our own knowledge and expertise and demonstrate a willingness to acknowledge those limitations both privately and publicly. For example, suppose you are about to meet with a client whose teenage daughter struggles with chronic fatigue and sleepiness. Imagine that you know virtually nothing about this topic. You might reflect the value of humility in learning if you were to say directly to the client, "I don't know much at all about chronic fatigue in adolescent girls. However, I am eager to locate someone who does."

Empathy Social workers reflect the value of empathy in learning when we conscientiously seek to discover and consider the experiences and perspectives of other people—especially those most affected by the topic or issue at hand. For example, suppose you are a social worker whose family migrated from Mexico 20 years earlier. Imagine that you have begun to work with several members of a Jordanian family who have recently immigrated to the United States. You might reflect the value of empathy in learning by recognizing that, although the memories of your own immigration might heighten your sensitivity to your clients' experiences, you still need to learn a great deal about Jordanian culture and especially the relocation experiences of this particular family.

Fairness Social workers reflect the value of fairness in learning when we consciously and conscientiously manage our personal tendencies toward egocentric, ethnocentric, and prejudicial thinking. To be fair in learning about a topic, social workers must exercise remarkable personal control. As human beings, we tend to maintain our beliefs even when faced with evidence that challenges or even refutes them. As social workers, many of us also underestimate the extent of our "intellectual or ideological conflicts of interest" that can interfere with learning.

For example, suppose you are a social worker whose political views tend to be distinctly liberal in nature. Imagine as well that you serve a large number of clients who are trying to disengage from governmentally sponsored support programs to become economically self-sufficient. To serve them well, you would like to locate intervention approaches shown to be effective in helping families achieve economic independence while sustaining or improving their psychosocial and physical well-being. By remaining open to and searching comprehensively for research studies about the effectiveness of local, state, and privately funded programs as well as federal programs, you reflect fairness. You would also reflect the values of fairness by searching for studies about interventions conducted by natural helpers, volunteers, and paraprofessionals, as well as by social workers and other professionals. In exercising the value of fairness, you conscientiously remain open to the possibility that nonfederal and even nonprofessional programs may be more effective than those you might prefer on the basis of your political views alone. By managing your personal beliefs, feelings, and your real as well as your intellectual conflicts of interest, you reflect the value of fairness in learning.

Courage Social workers reflect courage in learning when we reflect a consistent willingness to consider fully the documentary evidence that supports ideas, perspectives, and conclusions that are unpopular, unconventional, or different from our own. In particular, we manifest intellectual courage when we personally and publicly challenge false, misleading, or unsubstantiated assertions.

For example, suppose you serve as a social worker in a clinic for persons with HIV/AIDS and their families and friends. Because of the social stigma sometimes associated with this disease, you might need to call on considerable personal courage to confront accusations by others who possess limited understanding or compassion for your clients.

Honesty and Integrity   Social workers demonstrate honesty when we tell the truth and share valid information. We demonstrate integrity when we publicly acknowledge personal opinions and distinguish them from research-supported professional judgments and recommendations. We reflect integrity when we readily hold ourselves accountable to high intellectual and professional standards; when we voluntarily acknowledge mistakes and errors in our own thoughts, words, and deeds; and when we change our views based on scholarly evidence and the reasoned arguments of others. We reflect honesty when we acknowledge publicly the scholarly contributions of others and when we credit sources of information used to support our own statements and positions.

For example, suppose you serve as a social worker–lobbyist who advocates for progressive social policies within a state legislature. You would, of course, carefully and comprehensively search for valid and reliable information on which to base your policy recommendations to voting politicians. Suppose you locate evidence that calls into serious question the potential value of a policy you have supported and advocated. You would demonstrate honesty and integrity by acknowledging all the relevant facts and information—both pro and con—despite your role and personal biases.

Clarity, Precision, and Accuracy   Social workers display clarity, precision, and accuracy through our written and spoken statements, opinions, assertions, arguments, conclusions, and hypotheses. We communicate simply, clearly, and directly. We try to avoid obfuscation and reduce misunderstanding through the accurate and precise use of words. We often provide examples and illustrations to enhance understanding.

For example, suppose you are about to deliver a formal presentation at a national conference attended by social workers from all arenas of the profession. In presenting your material, you are keenly aware that members of the audience might indeed view you as an expert authority in the field. Thus, some of them might change the nature of their service to clients based on information you present. Therefore, you would want to reflect the highest standards of professional scholarship and communicate in a manner that is clear, accurate, and precise.

Relevance   Social workers demonstrate relevance when our learning plans, activities, and products bear upon the question or topic under consideration. Every effort is made to maintain focus on the problem, issue, or goal. In maintaining relevance, social workers avoid temptations to move to irrelevant, more easily grasped, or previously learned material.

For example, suppose a clinical social worker has a client who clearly manifests the symptoms of agoraphobia. The social worker is highly experienced in a person-centered approach to counseling but knows that the client would probably be much better served through cognitive-behavioral strategies that include graduated exposure. She does not know as much about this approach and will have to learn more, seek supervision or consultation, or perhaps refer the client to another professional. Although the social worker might be tempted to serve the agoraphobic client via the therapeutic method with which she is most familiar, she reflects relevance by focusing on the client's right to receive the most effective service.

Intellectual Sophistication Social workers demonstrate intellectual sophistication when we make statements that adequately reflect the relative complexity of the topic at hand. We consider all pertinent perspectives and reliable sources of information to describe issues in a balanced manner at the depth or breadth needed for genuine understanding. We address routine matters in a simple, straightforward manner and consider highly complex, multidimensional issues in an intellectually sophisticated manner. Social workers avoid overly simplistic analyses of complex topics and issues.

For example, imagine that the father of a 12-year-old anorexic girl asks you, "Should I make a big fuss about this or should I ignore it when she refuses to eat her meals?" If you were to reply as if these were the only possible responses to this complex situation, you would reflect intellectual naiveté rather than sophistication.

Logic Social workers reflect logic when our statements genuinely make good sense. We present coherent arguments that logically follow from stated premises and documentary evidence. And we base our conclusions on the reasonableness of the arguments and the quality of the supporting evidence. In manifesting logic, social workers recognize and manage the temptation to adopt common logical fallacies such as selective or biased use of evidence, begging the question, ad hominem attack, appeal to emotion, anecdotal experience, and straw man, slippery slope, or scare tactic reasoning (Engel, 1990; Gambrill, 1990, 1997; Gibbs & Gambrill, 1996; Gibbs, 1991, 1994; Moore & Parker, 1995).

Social worker students and practitioners that reflect these principles in learning are better prepared to serve clients in contemporary society. Social work practice based on continuous learning is consistent with motives of compassion, social justice, and altruism. Lifelong learning is also congruent with the core values and ethics of the social work profession. Indeed, in some circumstances, failure to learn about emerging research findings related to practice effectiveness and failure to apply them in service could constitute professional negligence or malpractice.

During the early portion of the 21st century, social workers increasingly experience the dual pressures of competition and accountability. By engaging actively in learning related to the needs and services of your clientele and communities, you should be well prepared to meet these expectations and simultaneously enhance your "employability quotient" and your value to your organization. Most important, however, by adopting an active, self-directed, and collaborative lifelong learning approach to your practice and profession, you will undoubtedly provide better quality services to the clients you serve.

Guidelines for Collaborative Group Learning in Social Work

Propelled by the third wave changes in society, spurred by the adult learning movement, and encouraged by the learning paradigm, each year more and more professors adopt methods such as "cooperative learning" (Cooper, 1995; Putnam, 1997), "collaborative learning" (Bosworth & Hamilton, 1994), "experiential learning" (Kolb, 1984), "problem based learning" (McBurney, 1995), "self-directed learning," "group learning" (Garside, 1996), "online learning" (Johnstone & Krauth, 1996; Leavitt, 1997), and "service learning"(Bringle & Hatcher, 1996; Enos & Troppe,

1996). Many of these innovative approaches to teaching and learning reflect similar premises about the characteristics of learners and the elements of effective learning. Several models use small group methods where students collaborate on projects that enable them to master course content and simultaneously develop skills for lifelong learning. Groups, however, constitute challenging learning contexts. Participants must be especially responsible and considerate of their colleagues. The demands are considerable. To facilitate collaborative group learning, we propose the following guidelines for membership and participation:

1. Group members commit to the principle that all participants have a great deal to offer and should have an approximately equal opportunity to contribute.
   a. Talkative, expressive learners commit to resist temptations to take more than their fair share of time and agree to assume responsibility for including others in the group process.
   b. Quiet, reflective learners commit to share more than they might normally share to contribute as full participants.
2. Group members commit to respect others as unique individuals, to value the right of people to hold or reach different views and perspectives, and to honor members' prerogative to change their minds.
   a. Participants agree to listen carefully to the comments of others, making sure that their words are accurately understood before expressing their own opinions.
3. Group members commit to a search for the most valid, reasonable, relevant, and reliable information upon which to base conclusions, opinions, hypotheses, and recommendations.
4. Group members commit to put in an approximately equal amount of time and effort in independent or cooperative searches for the best information and in the processes associated with critical analysis or application.
5. Group members commit to engage in learning activities and prepare learning products that deserve "quality" ratings of "good" or "excellent."[2]
   a. *Good quality* learning activities and products are characterized by competence in scholarship, critical and reflective thinking, and performance. Verbal presentations and written materials are well prepared. They reflect clarity, precision, good reasoning, and considerable insight. Intellectual standards of advanced scholarship are reflected in communications. A good quality rating suggests performance that is more than satisfactory. All basic expectations are met and some are exceeded. Self-assessment and self-evaluation are generally apparent. A number of significant issues are raised. Higher order thinking (analysis, synthesis, and evaluation) is usually reflected when topics and claims are explored. Major terms and concepts are usually clarified, assumptions are generally recognized, claims are typically supported with evidence, and arguments are usually presented in a fair and scholarly manner.
   b. *Excellent quality* learning activities and products are characterized by exceptional scholarship, analysis, and performance. Verbal presentations and written materials are extremely well prepared. Communications are clear, precise, well reasoned, and insightful. Intellectual standards of advanced scholarship are consistently reflected in verbal and written communications. A rating of excellence reflects work distinctly superior to that characterized as average, satisfactory, or good. All basic expectations are exceeded. Self-

---

[2]The Critical Thinking Community at www.criticalthinking.org/ contains much useful information related to both critical thinking and the assessment of learning products and activities.

assessment and self-evaluation are consistently apparent in excellent learning products and activities. The most significant issues are considered in depth. Higher order thinking (analysis, synthesis, and evaluation) in exploring topics and claims is consistently reflected. Major terms and concepts are routinely clarified, assumptions are recognized, claims are consistently supported with evidence, and arguments are always presented in a fair and scholarly manner.

6. Group members commit to incorporate means to assess the quality, effectiveness, relevance, and value of the collaborative learning experiences.

Contemporary approaches to education tend to reflect the view that most people are capable of taking a great deal of initiative in their own learning. Active learning and collaborative group experiences (Sutherland & Bonwell, 1996), in which students apply concepts and principles to case situations, analyze actual problems, or plan and implement activities designed to accomplish real-world goals, are becoming more common. In effect, most educational institutions are in the midst of a revolution that influences how we approach learning for social work. The social work portfolio that you plan, prepare, assess, and revise constitutes an important part of this revolution.

Increased competition and heightened demands for accountability, along with the changes accompanying the information age and the learning revolution, are dramatically affecting social workers and their clients. To address these trends, we have prepared this small book to help you prepare a social work portfolio and develop skills for lifelong learning. We invite learners of all kinds—those called teachers or professors as well as those called students or graduates—to embrace these initiatives to prepare social workers who can provide the highest quality service to clients during the early part of the 21st century. Indeed, by learning how to learn continuously throughout your professional lifetime, you will be better prepared to help clients become lifelong learners as well. The social work portfolio is intended to help you plan, assess, and document learning during your academic program and throughout your professional career.

Exercises

Toward the end of each chapter, we ask you to undertake various learning exercises. We hope they help you prepare an excellent social work portfolio and encourage your growth as an active, self-directed, and collaborative lifelong learner. Some of the exercises emphasize independent forms of learning, and others encourage group experiences. Many involve brief writing exercises to enhance your written communication skills and improve your critical thinking abilities. We believe that these forms of learning are essential for contemporary social work.

Independent Learning Exercises

Working independently, please complete the following learning exercises. Some of these exercises will help you prepare your social work portfolio; others will contribute to the development of lifelong learning skills.

1.1 In a paragraph or so, describe your initial reactions to the idea of a social work portfolio for use during your academic program and throughout your professional career. Please word process your response and save it to a computer diskette or hard drive. Name the file in a way that you can readily associate it with this exercise (e.g., Portfolio Exercise 1.1).

1.2 Think critically about the knowledge explosion, the information age, and the learning revolution. Then go to Appendix 1 and complete the Lifelong Learning Questionnaire. Reflect upon your responses to the items in the questionnaire. Following that, discuss in a two- or three-paragraph essay how the rapid pace of change in knowledge and information may affect you as a student, a lifelong learner, and a professional social worker. Then identify three to five competencies you could develop or enhance to become and remain an active, independent, and collaborative lifelong learner and effective professional social worker during this time of continuous change. Word process your short essay. Save and label the file.

1.3 In another short essay, discuss how a well-prepared social work portfolio might help you develop the competencies you identified in Exercise 1.2. Word process the essay and save the file.

1.4 Reflect upon and think critically about the principles for lifelong learning in social work. In a word-processed paragraph or so, describe your reactions to these guidelines. Discuss which principles might be most challenging for you to implement. Save the file.

Collaborative Group Learning Exercises

Form a small group of four to six social work student colleagues.[3] The primary purpose of the group is to help the participants become better learners, learn something of value, and work toward the development of high-quality social work portfolios. Assume that you will work and learn together for a considerable length of time—perhaps several weeks, months, a year, or possibly throughout your entire academic program. Introduce yourselves and share pertinent contact information.

1.5 Following the introductions, review and discuss with your colleagues the principles for lifelong learning in social work and the guidelines for collaborative group learning presented earlier in the chapter. Work toward consensus about the guiding principles for your collaborative learning group. Make note of areas of agreement and disagreement, along with themes that emerge during the discussion.

1.6 Take a moment to review your responses to the independent learning exercises that concerned the knowledge explosion, the information age, the heightened demands for quality and accountability, and the learning revolution within institutions of higher education. Identify one or two issues that strike you as particularly noteworthy. Discuss these with your colleagues. Make note of the major themes and issues that arise during the conversation.

1.7 Assume that collaborative group experiences will increasingly be part of modern approaches to learning both during your university studies and following graduation. Discuss the potential benefits and drawbacks to group learning activities. Address pertinent issues, including the question of fairness and equity. For example, explore what could or should happen if one or more group members do not fully participate in activities, contribute inequitably, or serve to obstruct the group's efforts and members' overall learning. Similarly, discuss how you might recognize and reward members who generously provide much more than expected.

1.8 Initiate a general discussion with your colleagues about the social work portfolio and its potential relevance for lifelong learning and contemporary professional practice. Identify the needs and potential motivating forces that might encourage you to engage in active, self-

---

[3] In some contexts, a course instructor may assign or facilitate the formation of collaborative learning groups. In others, an adviser or program coordinator may aid in the group composition process. In others, students may be encouraged to form their own collaborative learning or "study" groups.

directed, independent, and collaborative lifelong learning activities and to prepare and maintain a portfolio. Discuss the potential obstacles that could impede learning in your academic program and later during your professional social work career. Share your thoughts about how your collaborative learning group might facilitate or complicate your attempts at learning. Discuss how the group members might help each other prepare high-quality social work portfolios. Make note of major themes, issues, and observations that emerge during the discussions. Subsequently, reflect upon the group session, identify what you learned, and target areas that you would like to explore further. In a short summary essay, word process your thoughts, observations, and reflections. Save them in a computer file.

EXPLORING YOUR LEARNING SELF

What kind of learner are you? Do you like to work independently, read scholarly books, and listen carefully to experts in a field? Do you enjoy group discussions about topics and issues and learn through those conversations? Might you prefer to learn by doing, perhaps through trial and error in an applied experiment that you work at diligently until you get it right? Do you like to think things through carefully and reflect upon the potential implications and consequences of various perspectives before expressing your viewpoint or taking action? As humans, we vary in the way we approach learning. We do not all learn in the same way, at the same pace, or even in the same places.

In this chapter (see Box 2.1), we help you become more aware of your characteristics and qualities as a learner. You will learn about your various intelligences, including emotional intelligence, your psychological type, and your preferred learning style and preferences. We hope that enhanced awareness of your learning self will help you become an active, self-directed, and collaborative learner during your academic studies and afterward as a practicing professional. We also believe that increased self-awareness will aid you in the preparation of a high-quality social work portfolio for use in effectively pursuing your career aspirations and learning goals.

The social work profession encompasses a wide range of functions and activities. Social work takes place in various contexts with diverse peoples and communities. It is challenging work that requires a great deal of knowledge, skills, and commitment to a core set of values. As a result, learning for social work cannot be limited to a narrow range or conception of knowledge. Social workers must develop attitudinally, emotionally, and interpersonally as well as intellectually. Learning must reflect breadth, depth, and growth as social workers provide new services in different contexts to new or different peoples and communities. Indeed, the nature, focus, and purposes for your learning are likely to change over time as you proceed through the various stages of your professional career.[1]

Contemporary Perspectives on Learning

The rapidly changing demographic, socioeconomic, and technological forces in modern society require that social workers learn, unlearn, and relearn quickly, efficiently, and effectively. Contemporary social workers need to adapt rapidly to increasingly varied and complex demands on their knowledge, values, and skills. We must engage in lifelong learning to cope adequately with the social and professional challenges of the 21st century.

The concept of lifelong learning and continuing education as essential components of ongoing professional development is of fairly recent origin. During the first half of the 20th century,

---

[1] Appendix 2 contains an outline of common phases of a professional social work career. You may wish to refer to it as you consider your own career development.

BOX

2.1   **CHAPTER PURPOSE**

The primary purpose of this chapter is to enhance awareness of your learning self. You will learn about multiple intelligences, emotional intelligence, psychological type, and learning style as they relate to your approach to learning. Such self-awareness should help you prepare a high-quality social work portfolio and, more important, contribute to your development as an active, self-directed, and collaborative lifelong learner.

Goals

Following completion of this chapter, you should be able to:

- Describe your qualities and characteristics as a learner
- Discuss the topics of multiple intelligences, emotional intelligence, psychological type, and learning style as they apply to your learning self
- Identify dimensions of your learning self that you want to strengthen
- Use your growing awareness of your learning self to plan a high-quality social work portfolio

---

a university-based education was generally considered sufficient preparation for an entire career. Some theorists even wondered whether middle-aged and older adults could truly benefit from educational opportunities in their advanced years. A number of modern researchers, however, questioned the belief that intellectual capacity diminishes as people age. Older age does not represent as much of an obstacle to learning as previously believed (Lohman, 1989). Most people have the capacity to learn new and different material throughout their entire lifetimes. Indeed, in recent years, the concept of intelligence itself has undergone a radical transformation.

Multiple Intelligences

During much of the 20th century, professionals in Western societies tended to view intelligence in a fairly narrow manner. A numerical score received on a standardized intelligence (IQ) test was often perceived as a reasonably accurate indicator of intellectual capacity. More recently, however, this view has come under serious challenge. Some researchers suggest that intelligence includes multiple dimensions that extend well beyond what is usually reflected by traditional IQ tests. For example, Howard Gardner (1983, 1993, 1999) postulated the existence of some eight multiple intelligences. Each of these various types of intelligence denotes the ability or capacity to develop and learn in that designated area. If we extrapolate each of Gardner's multiple intelligences to social workers, we might observe the following characteristics:

- *Verbal–Linguistic*: Verbal-linguistic intelligence reflects the ability to use words accurately and articulately. Social workers who possess strength in verbal-linguistic intelligence probably enjoy reading, writing, and speaking. They might enjoy writing letters, reports, articles, or books. They might like to give talks or make speeches.
- *Logical–Mathematical*: Logical–mathematical intelligence reflects the ability to use numerical systems and processes accurately and effectively. Social workers who possess strength in logical–mathematical intelligence might be curious about classifications, categories, patterns, sequences, and relationships among components. They probably enjoy the

intellectual processes of analysis, assessment, diagnosis, and planning. They might also appreciate scientific experimentation and mathematical or statistical problem solving.

- *Bodily–Kinesthetic*: Bodily–kinesthetic intelligence reflects the ability to use one's body precisely and productively. Social workers who possess strength in bodily-kinesthetic intelligence probably seek and process information through bodily sensations and movement. They might enjoy sports, recreational activities, dancing, and artistic and handicraft activities.
- *Visual–Spatial*: Visual–spatial intelligence reflects the ability to perceive and generate shapes and spaces precisely. Social workers who possess strength in visual–spatial intelligence probably process information visually. They might readily form mental pictures and use those pictures as they attempt to understand some issue or problem. They might enjoy mental challenges that involve visual and spatial dimensions. They might find themselves daydreaming often and enjoy drawing or doodling.
- *Musical–Rhythmical*: Musical–rhythmical intelligence reflects the ability to appreciate, understand, and incorporate rhythm in daily activities. Social workers who possess strength in musical intelligence probably seek and process information aurally and rhythmically. They might hum, whistle, drum, or sing as they do other things. They are probably good listeners and may notice sounds that other people do not.
- *Interpersonal*: Interpersonal intelligence reflects the ability to understand and to relate positively and effectively with other people. Social workers who possess strength in interpersonal intelligence are probably empathic listeners, effective communicators, and natural leaders. They tend to be sociable people who interact comfortably and easily with others.
- *Intrapersonal*: Intrapersonal intelligence reflects the ability to form an accurate and complete understanding of oneself and to use such self-knowledge effectively. Social workers who possess strength in intrapersonal intelligence are probably thoughtful and reflective. They tend to be extremely aware of their own thoughts, feelings, and motives. They are probably highly self-motivated.
- *Naturalist*: Naturalist intelligence reflects the abilities to observe and categorize aspects of the natural environment or ecology. Social workers who possess strength in naturalist intelligence are probably observant of their surroundings. They might be especially sensitive to changes in aspects of the environment such as weather, geography, architecture, and various forms of life (e.g., plant, animal, and human) within the ecology. They tend to be extremely aware of their natural and social environment.

Multifaceted views of intelligence may be useful to people generally as they prepare for and engage in learning during their university studies and throughout their lives. Social workers in particular may find the theory of multiple intelligences especially useful for both themselves and their clients. We believe that many members of society's most vulnerable populations have been unfairly limited by narrow views of intellectual capacity and potential. By extending the scope of intelligence to include several dimensions, you may help clients more accurately assess their own strengths, abilities, and capacities. You may also do the same for yourself. You may even discover aspects of your own intelligence that you have not previously recognized.

Emotional Intelligence

Salovey and Mayer (1990; Mayer & Salovey, 1997) and Goleman (1995) also expanded the traditional concept of intelligence to include the dimension of emotions. Goleman contended that emotional intelligence involves "abilities such as being able to motivate oneself and persist in the face of frustrations; to control impulse and delay gratification; to regulate one's moods and keep distress from swamping the ability to think; to empathize and to hope" (1995, p. 34). These qualities tend to develop in the early years of life. Emotional abilities acquired later in life build on these early foundations.

Emotions undoubtedly have great value and utility for human beings and contribute to the survival of the species. According to Goleman, the capacity for learning and understanding "how to learn" are both related to emotional intelligence. He defined emotion as "a feeling and its distinctive thoughts, psychological and biological states, and range of propensities to act. There are hundreds of emotions, along with their blends, variations, mutations, and nuances" (1995, p. 289).

Goleman suggested that human emotions serve as important and powerful guides to action. Consider the example of a woman who has never learned to swim. She carefully watches her young daughter swim in a small lake. Her daughter begins to struggle, coughs several times, and then screams as she sinks beneath the surface. Unable to swim, the woman nonetheless jumps in and somehow stays afloat long enough to pull her drowning daughter to safety. Later she wonders how she could possibly accomplish what she did. Although we cannot be certain of all the contributing factors, it may be that aspects of her emotional intelligence took control of her rational mind and motivated her to heroic action.

Most of the time, our emotions guide us in more subtle ways. In general, they serve us well. Often, for example, our feelings serve to signal us that we need to attend to some issue within our lives. Sometimes, however, they represent obstacles or barriers to overcome and powerful forces to control. Awareness of emotions and our propensities to act on them as well as the ability to manage them are advantageous to most people. We believe that well-developed emotional intelligence is, quite simply, indispensable for social workers. We cannot conceive of circumstances where the lack of emotional self-awareness or absence of emotional control would help a social worker effectively serve clients.

As Goleman has suggested, there may be hundreds of emotions. Certainly, they have not all been identified or classified. However, there seem to be certain natural families of emotions. Goleman (1995) clusters them in this fashion:

- *Anger*: fury, outrage, resentment, wrath, exasperation, indignation, vexation, acrimony, animosity, annoyance, irritability, hostility, and, perhaps at the extreme, pathological hatred and violence
- *Sadness*: grief, sorrow, cheerlessness, gloom, melancholy, self-pity, loneliness, dejection, despair, and when pathological, severe depression
- *Fear*: anxiety, apprehension, nervousness, concern, consternation, misgiving, wariness, qualm, edginess, dread, fright, terror; as a psychopathology, phobia and panic
- *Enjoyment*: happiness, joy, relief, contentment, bliss, delight, amusement, pride, sensual pleasure, thrill, rapture, gratification, satisfaction, euphoria, whimsy, ecstasy, and at the far edge, mania
- *Love*: acceptance, friendliness, trust, kindness, affinity, devotion, adoration, infatuation, agape

- *Surprise*: shock, astonishment, amazement, wonder
- *Disgust*: contempt, disdain, scorn, abhorrence, aversion, distaste, revulsion
- *Shame*: guilt, embarrassment, chagrin, remorse, humiliation, regret, mortification, and contrition. (pp. 289–290)[2]

Humans vary in the relative strength and distribution of these families of emotions. Some people find it difficult to identify, experience, or express any emotion. Others have ready access to a wide range of emotions and express them easily and intensely. Some individuals experience high levels of one family of emotions, perhaps anger or shame, and rarely feel others. Needless to say, there is wide variation from person to person and culture to culture in terms of emotional experience, expressiveness, and control.

It does seem clear, however, that people who have learned to access, manage, and express their emotions selectively are better prepared to function effectively in social circumstances. This does not surprise social workers. We have long helped people strengthen their psychosocial self-management capacities through activities such as counseling or psychotherapy, self-analysis, and reflection as well as programs such as anger management, assertiveness training, parent training, social skills development, and a host of related approaches. Nonetheless, the idea of specifically planned learning activities designed to heighten affective competence and strengthen emotional intelligence remains relatively uncommon. The notion, however, is profoundly intriguing for both social workers and their clients. Might becoming more emotionally intelligent and affectively adept help social workers better serve their clients? Similarly, might growth in this area contribute to clients' ability to identify, manage, and use their feelings in pursuit of their own goals and aspirations? We think so.

As described by Goleman (1998), the main components of such learning would probably include opportunities to develop the following kinds of emotional abilities or competencies:

1. Personal Competence: These competencies determine how we manage ourselves.
   a. Self-Awareness: Know one's internal states, preferences, resources, and intuitions
      i. Emotional awareness: Recognizing one's emotions and their effects
      ii. Accurate self-assessment: Knowing one's strengths and limits
      iii. Self-confidence: A strong sense of one's self-worth and capabilities
   b. Self-Regulation: Managing one's internal states, impulses, and resources
      i. Self-Control: Keeping disruptive emotions and impulses in check
      ii. Trustworthiness: Maintaining standards of honesty and integrity
      iii. Conscientiousness: Taking responsibility for personal performance
      iv. Adaptability: Flexibility in handling change
      v. Innovation: Being comfortable with novel ideas, approaches, and new information
   c. Motivation: Emotional tendencies that guide or facilitate reaching goals
      i. Achievement drive: Striving to improve or meet a standard of excellence
      ii. Commitment: Aligning with the goals of the group or organization
      iii. Initiative: Readiness to act on opportunities
      iv. Optimism: Persistence in pursuing goals despite obstacles and setbacks
2. Social Competence: These competencies determine how we handle relationships.

---

[2] From *Emotional Intelligence* by Daniel Goleman, copyright © 1995 by Daniel Goleman. Used by permission of Bantam Books, a division of Random House, Inc.

a. Empathy: Awareness of others' feelings, needs, and concerns
 i. Understanding others: Sensing others' feelings and perspectives, and taking an active interest in their concerns
 ii. Developing others: Sensing others' development needs and bolstering their abilities
 iii. Service orientation: Anticipating, recognizing, and meeting . . . [others'] [3] . . . needs
 iv. Leveraging diversity: Cultivating opportunities through different kinds of people
 v. Political awareness: Reading a group's emotional currents and power relationships
b. Social Skills: Adeptness at inducing desirable responses in others
 i. Influence: Wielding effective tactics for persuasion
 ii. Communication: Listening openly and sending convincing messages
 iii. Conflict management: Negotiating and resolving disagreements
 iv. Leadership: Inspiring and guiding individuals and groups
 v. Change catalyst: Initiating or managing change
 vi. Building bonds: Nurturing instrumental relationships
 vii. Collaboration and cooperation: Working with others toward shared goals
 viii. Team capabilities: Creating group synergy in pursuing collective goals. (pp. 26–27) [4]

As professional helpers, social workers must be competent in these intrapersonal and interpersonal abilities. A strong and growing emotional intelligence is crucial for a successful social work career. Of course, a perfect curriculum that everybody must or should learn to become and remain an emotionally intelligent and effective social worker does not exist. Indeed, success is only partially dependent on the course of study, the subject matter, or the conditions of learning. Individual characteristics such as personality, levels of interest, energy, motivation, and commitment vary. So do psychological type and learning style.

Psychological Type

Psychological type or temperament has been a major focus of study for many researchers in recent years. Several have addressed the relationship of psychological type to learning. Some have used the popular Myers-Briggs Type Indicator (MBTI) (Myers, 1962) in their studies. Isabel Briggs Myers and her mother, Katharine Cook Briggs, developed the MBTI instrument on the basis of Carl Jung's theory. The four dimensions of psychological type may be conceptualized on continua as follows:

- *Introversion (I) versus Extraversion (E)*: In general, people who generate energy through independent activities and periods of solitude usually reflect a preference for introversion. Those who derive positive energy from contact with other people tend to reflect a preference for extraversion. Among the general population of the United States, more people manifest an extraverted than an introverted style (Keirsey & Bates, 1984).
- *Intuition (N) versus Sensation (S)*: People who are innovative, abstract, metaphorical, and speculative tend to reflect a preference for intuition. Those who are practical, sensible, and

---

[3] Goleman used the term *customer* in his 1998 book *Working with Emotional Intelligence* (New York: Bantam Books). We believe the term *other* can be used here instead.

[4] From *Working with Emotional Intelligence* by Daniel Goleman, copyright © 1998 by Daniel Goleman. Used by permission of Bantam Books, a division of Random House, Inc.

realistic tend to reveal a preference for sensation. More Americans reflect a preference for sensation than for intuition.

- *Thinking (T) versus Feeling (F)*: People who prefer to make decisions on the basis of impersonal criteria reflect a preference for thinking. Those who make choices on the basis of unique circumstances and personal implications tend to reflect a feeling preference. Although approximately 50% of the U.S. population tends to prefer a thinking and half a feeling style, more men than women tend to reveal a preference for thinking, whereas more women than men prefer feeling.

- *Judging (J) versus Perceiving (P)*: People who like to make decisions, finish tasks, and generally reach closure fairly quickly tend to reflect a preference for judging. Those who like to wait a considerable length of time and collect additional information or consider alternate perspectives before reaching decisions or taking action tend to reflect a preference for perception. About 50% of the U.S. population reflect a judging style, whereas the other half reflect a perceiving style.

People generally reflect a preference for one direction on each of these four dimensions and may be characterized on that basis. These preferences tend to affect how people learn (Lawrence, 1994). For example, suppose two social workers have decided to collaborate on a project. The first social worker is more extraverted, and the other is more introverted. The first is more intuitive, and the second is more sensitive. The first is more thoughtful, and the second is more emotional. The first is more perceptive, and the other is more judging. The first social worker would be classified as an "extraverted, intuitive, thinking, perceiving" (ENTP) psychological type. The other would be classified as an "introverted, sensation, feeling, judging" (ISFJ) type. These are contrasting profiles. Thus, the two social workers would probably approach the task in distinctly different ways. They would also tend to adopt different styles in their pursuit of learning opportunities and activities. These differences could either facilitate or impede completion of the project depending on how they view and adapt to one another's styles.

Within this system, there are 16 possible psychological types (see Table 2.1). Research has yielded common personal characteristics associated with each type, along with the approximate percentage of the American population that falls into each category (Keirsey & Bates, 1984). Psychological type affects how people approach and experience learning. For example, extraverted learners may tend to value spontaneous, wide-ranging conversations, whereas introverted learners might prefer individual study or time for reflection prior to discussions that focus on the topics at hand.

The Myers-Briggs Type Indicator is a psychological assessment instrument usually administered by a certified professional. Other authors have developed similar scales or inventories for the assessment of psychological type or style. David Keirsey and Marilyn Bates (1984), for example, devised a self-administered scale called the Temperament Sorter that yields MBTI-like classifications.

Keirsey believed that Plato, Aristotle, Fromm, Myers, and others were correct in their observations that human beings reflect four fundamental temperaments. Keirsey (1998) adopted Plato's classifications of artisan, guardian, idealist, and rational and referred to the 16 psychological types to organize them (see Table 2.1).

According to Keirsey, artisans (SP) manifest strength within the sensing (S) and perceiving (P) dimensions. Drawn to excitement, experience, and adventure, artisans tend to learn best

TABLE 2.1 **16 PSYCHOLOGICAL TYPES ORGANIZED BY CORE TEMPERAMENTS**

Artisans Sensing–Perceiving	Guardians Sensing–Judging	Idealists Intuitive–Feeling	Rationals Intuitive–Thinking
ISFP (6%)	ISFJ (6%)	INFP (1%)	INTP (1%)
ESFP (13%)	ESFJ (13%)	ENFP (5%)	ENTP (5%)
ISTP (6%)	ISTJ (6%)	INFJ (1%)	INTJ (1%)
ESTP (13%)	ESTJ (13%)	ENFJ (5%)	ENTJ (5%)
Total SP (38%)	**Total SJ (38%)**	**Total NF (12%)**	**Total NT (12%)**

Note: Approximate percent of U.S. population in each type presented in parentheses.

Sources: Keirsey, D., & Bates, M. (1984). *Please understand me: Character and temperament types.* (4th ed.). Del Mar, CA: Prometheus Nemesis; and Tieger, P. D., & Barron-Tieger, B. (1992). *Do what you are: Discover the perfect career for you through the secrets of psychological type.* Boston: Little, Brown.

through active, experiential, hands-on learning. They often enjoy competition and some risk. Simulations, role-plays, and educational contests of various kinds can engage the SP learner. Guardians (SJ) reflect ability within the sensing (S) and judging (J) dimensions. Thus, they tend toward the traditional and predictable. They often work hard in both cooperative and independent contexts and respond well to guidance and direction. SJ learners value clear and specific tasks and expectations. Idealists (NF) reflect strength in the intuitive (N) and feeling (F) dimensions. Often searching for a sense of uniqueness and identity, NF learners tend to prefer cooperative, cordial group learning within a friendly context. Sometimes sensitive to criticism, idealists enjoy exercising their imaginations and exploring possibilities. Rationals (NT) display potential within the intuitive (N) and thinking (T) dimensions. NT learners seek to understand and explain. Competence, logical analysis, objectivity, and empirical research tend to be highly valued. Rationals tend to enjoy independent study and often learn best through investigation, experimentation, and in-depth library research. Group learning activities may be somewhat challenging for NT learners (Lawrence, 1994).

Learning Style

The topic of learning style has been addressed in other ways as well. For example, David A. Kolb studied experiential learning (1984, 1999; Kolb, Osland, & Rubin, 1994; Kolb, Rubin, & Osland, 1994) and proposed a two-dimensional model to illustrate various learning styles. The dimensions are (a) concrete experience (CE) versus abstract conceptualization (AC) and (b) active experimentation (AE) versus reflective observation (RO). Four core styles emerge from the two-dimensional matrix. Kolb (1984) described the four as divergent (CE/RO), assimilative (AC/RO), convergent (AC/AE), and accommodative (CE/AE). He suggested that people tend to reflect a preferred learning style and learn more effectively and efficiently when learning opportunities are presented in ways that match their style. In outlining these preferred styles, however, Kolb noted that people use all four approaches at various times. He cautioned that the discrete styles should never be viewed as fixed or static traits. Rather, they are preferred, but not exclusive, styles by which people tend to approach and experience learning.

For example, suppose a group of four social work students plans to learn how to use an electronic mail (e-mail) system. Assume that each of the students reflects a distinct preference for one of Kolb's core learning styles. As a group, they manifest all four styles. In approaching the learning task, the following characteristics might be observed:

- *Diverging*: Diverging learners like to understand why the information is needed and how it will help them. The diverging learner might be interested to know why one e-mail system is better than another and might like to have supporting documentation or evidence.
- *Assimilating*: Assimilating learners tend to be curious. They like to learn new information. They tend to be fascinated by ideas, concepts, and theories. The assimilating learner probably reads technical manuals and might attend workshops to learn as much as possible about the system.
- *Converging*: Converging learners like to apply what they have learned. They seek to put learning into action. Through applied experience, they test the utility of the knowledge. The converging learner probably experiments with the e-mail system and learns through trial and error.
- *Accommodating*: Accommodating learners want to know how their learning will make a difference. They seek to have an impact on others and on the world at large. They generally enjoy working and mixing with other people. Group activities tend to be pleasurable and satisfying. They often serve as group leaders. The accommodating learner would invite others to join in a group to learn about the system and might quickly use e-mail to facilitate communication among members.

Kolb and others have popularized the concept of a learning cycle or learning wheel (Handy, 1989). Similar to the Shewhart or PDSA Cycle (i.e., Plan-Do-Study-Act) that was introduced by Deming (1986), the steps or processes are *reflecting* (i.e., observing your own thoughts and behavior—often as a part of self-assessment), *connecting* (i.e., thinking about what might be done—based on the results of the reflecting stage—and generating a range of potential action steps), *deciding* (i.e., selecting one or more action steps from those identified in the connecting stage), and *doing* (i.e., undertaking the planned action steps) (Senge, Kleiner, Roberts, Ross, & Smith, 1994, p. 60). The learning wheel is conceptualized as an ongoing process where reflecting follows doing (i.e., you think about the processes and outcomes associated with the doing stage), connecting follows reflecting, deciding follows connecting, doing follows deciding, and reflecting again follows doing. Ideally, the learning cycle continues ad infinitum.

Richard Felder has also considered the topic of learning styles. He reviewed, analyzed, and synthesized several theories and the results of various research studies (Herrmann, 1990; Kolb, 1984; Lawrence, 1994) to propose an integrative model (Felder & Silverman, 1988). Although originally intended for students in the basic sciences, his model may be effectively applied to social workers as well. As with other learners, social workers reflect a range of learning style preferences.

Felder's integrated model includes five learning style dimensions: (a) active–reflective, (b) sensing–intuitive, (c) visual–verbal, (d) inductive–deductive, and (e) sequential–global. These dimensions are continuous rather than dichotomous and dynamic rather than static. Certainly, most of us learn more easily when the learning activities match our learning style. However, people probably benefit from engagement in multistyle learning activities. We can develop strength in other styles of learning when we challenge ourselves to learn in ways that are less familiar and "natural."

Here are brief descriptions of the polar extremes of each of the five dimensions:

- *Active–Reflective Styles*: According to Felder and Solomon (2000), people at the active pole of the active–reflective continuum tend to learn best when they do something with the material they seek to learn. For example, they might attempt to solve a problem, teach another person, or apply it to an issue. They like to experiment, and trial-and-error approaches hold considerable appeal. Active learners often enjoy working within group contexts. Those at the reflective pole of the dimension prefer to think about, reflect upon, and internally consider the information before taking action. For instance, they might prefer to theorize about the potential implications of the material before applying it to a problem or conducting an experiment. Reflective learners often enjoy time for solitary reflection before they begin a group learning activity.

- *Sensing–Intuitive Styles*: People at the sensing end of the sensing–intuitive dimension prefer factual information and often enjoy detailed material. They typically tend to prefer predictable, replicable means of analysis and application. Often meticulous and reliable, sensing learners may reflect excellent "common sense" and can easily remember facts, figures, routines, and protocols. Those at the intuitive pole tend to enjoy theoretical material, including abstract concepts. They often think quickly and creatively and frequently adapt or extend ideas or principles into new areas.

- *Visual–Verbal*: Within the visual–verbal continuum, visual learners tend to learn best through images of various kinds. "Sight" is the preferred mode of learning. Movies and videos, live enactments, and assorted graphic representations (e.g., charts, graphs) help visual learners understand and remember newly presented information. At the other pole, verbal learners tend to prefer language to images. Verbal learners enjoy both spoken and written language as a means of communication. Of course, most people—including visual and verbal learners—tend to learn best when new material is addressed in multidimensional ways so that both visual and verbal (reading and listening) modes are addressed.

- *Inductive–Deductive*: People at the inductive end of the inductive–deductive continuum tend to prefer to observe events, examine particular cases, or consider individual situations. Inductive learners like facts and details. Then, understanding the particulars, they proceed to develop or extrapolate general principles. Deductive learners, on the other hand, reflect a preference for rules, guidelines, principles, or theories. They enjoy abstract concepts. Then, understanding the general, they apply it to particular circumstances.

- *Sequential–Global*: Within the sequential–global dimension, sequential learners generally prefer to learn and address intellectual problems in logical, linear, A-B-C fashion. For example, sequential learners seem to enjoy logically constructed outlines that proceed in step-by-step fashion to a logical conclusion. Global learners tend to prefer getting the big picture and may approach topics from several different perspectives almost simultaneously. They may not immediately notice the stepwise or linear connections until they grasp the whole, at which time they may be able to fill in missing pieces quite easily.

We recognize and celebrate the proposition that people are not destined to remain strong in some and weak in other learning style dimensions or preferences. Indeed, we believe that most of us benefit when we are exposed to a variety of learning activities. Not only do people tend to learn better through multidimensional forms of learning, but in so doing, we also may strengthen attributes that have been underdeveloped.

Exercises

This chapter contains a good deal of information related to the topics of multiple intelligences, emotional intelligence, psychological type, and learning style. The following exercises may take some time to complete. As you did in Chapter 1, please word process your written responses to the independent learning exercises and, following the collaborative group learning exercises, word process your summary reactions as well. Label each computer file in an easily identifiable fashion (e.g., Portfolio Exercise 2.1).

Independent Learning Exercises

2.1 As Howard Gardner suggested, we believe that you have multiple intelligences. Log on to the World Wide Web and go to surfaquarium.com/MIinvent.htm. At that site, you will find a Multiple Intelligence Survey developed by Walter McKenzie. Instructions for scoring the survey are provided online, but you will have to calculate the score yourself. When you have finished, review the results. Reflect upon those intelligences where you show strength and those that appear less well developed. Consider other sources of information about your various intelligences (e.g., your experience, others' comments about your talents). Then, using information gained from all sources, prepare a brief word-processed essay (2–3 paragraphs) in which you discuss how your multiple intelligences' profile might influence your approach to learning. In particular, discuss how you might maximize your intelligences to enhance your learning potential as a social work student and future professional.

2.2 Go to the World Wide Web at www.utne.com/azEq2.tmpl to find a brief, informal test of emotional intelligence developed by Daniel Goleman. Complete the instrument online. Your score will be calculated automatically. Review the results. Also consider other sources of information about your emotional intelligence. Word process an essay about the implications of your current emotional intelligence for your performance as a student, a member of a collaborative learning group, a professional social worker, and a lifelong learner. In your discussion, describe how you might maximize your strengths and manage your weaknesses in several of the following areas:

- Your ability to recognize your own emotions and their associated effects
- Your ability to assess accurately your strengths and weaknesses
- Your sense of self-confidence, self-worth, and competence
- Your ability to manage your emotions and impulses
- Your ability to be responsible and honest when you might be tempted to be irresponsible or dishonest
- Your ability to take responsibility for your own actions, including mistakes and failures as well as achievements and successes
- Your ability to adapt to and cope with change
- Your ability to remain comfortable when presented with new or different facts, views, and opinions
- Your ability to work toward personal or professional goals
- Your ability to work toward the goals of the groups to which you belong
- Your ability to take initiative when opportunities occur
- Your ability to remain optimistic and continue to work toward the achievement of goals in the face of challenges and roadblocks

- Your ability to feel interest in other people and empathically understand and value their thoughts, feelings, and experiences
- Your ability to appreciate and support others in their personal and professional growth and development
- Your willingness to serve others by understanding, appreciating, and addressing their needs, wants, and preferences
- Your ability to appreciate, include, and value diverse individuals and groups
- Your ability to understand and assess the social and political dynamics within a group

2.3 Review the description of the psychological types assessed by the Myers-Briggs Type Indicator (MBTI) or the Keirsey Temperament Sorter. Your instructor, adviser, or university career counseling office may be able to help you access a copy of the MBTI. Or you may complete the latest version of the Keirsey instrument—The Keirsey Temperament Sorter II—online. The Web site address is www.keirsey.com. Your score will be calculated for you. You may also find the instrument along with scoring instructions in David Keirsey's 1998 book, *Please Understand Me II: Temperament, Character, Intelligence* (Del Mar, CA: Prometheus Nemesis).

When you have completed the MBTI or the Keirsey Temperament Sorter, review your psychological type profile and consider which of the four temperaments (artisan, idealist, guardian, or rational) best reflects your core characteristics. In a brief word-processed essay, discuss the implications of your psychological type for roles as a social work student, a member of a collaborative learning group, a professional social worker, and a lifelong learner.

2.4 Richard Felder has integrated several perspectives on learning style (Felder, 1993, pp. 286–287). He suggested that you may determine your preferred learning style by addressing these five questions:

a. Do you prefer to perceive information via the sensory (e.g., the senses of sight, hearing, feeling, taste, smell) or the intuitive mode (e.g., the cognitive experience of thoughts, ideas, recollections)?

b. Do you find that you learn and remember better when you perceive information visually (e.g., images, graphic representations, charts) or verbally (e.g., printed or spoken language)?

c. Do you find that you intellectually organize and understand information better through inductive (e.g., you derive the abstract concepts and principles from concrete details or experience) or through deductive processes (e.g., you apply the concepts and principles to the real world and hypothesize about the effects)?

d. Do you find that you are more likely to process information actively (e.g., you do something with the information) or reflectively (e.g., you intellectually consider and introspectively ponder the meaning and implications of the information)?

e. Do you find that you are able to reach a genuine understanding of information when you explore it sequentially (e.g., through a logical, linear, small step-by-step process) or globally (e.g., through an analogical, multidimensional, holistic overview)?

Your responses to these questions should help you gain a beginning sense of your learning style preferences on these five dimensions. To develop a more sophisticated self-understanding, however, we suggest that you complete the 44-item Index of Learning Styles (ILS) (Felder & Solomon, 2000). The ILS may be taken and scored online at www.crc4mse.org/ILS/Index.html. (It is also reprinted in Appendix 3 of this book.) Based on the Felder integrated model, the ILS represents an extremely promising tool for identifying learners' relative strengths on four of the five learning style dimensions: active–reflective, sensing–intuitive, visual–verbal, and sequential–global. The current version of the instrument does not assess strength on the inductive–deductive dimension.

Following completion of the ILS, please consider your results in terms of the relative strength on the four dimensions. Word process a short essay in which you discuss the implications of these findings for yourself as a social work student, a member of a collaborative learning group, a professional social worker, and a lifelong learner.

Collaborative Group Learning Exercises

Before initiating the group exercises, be sure to take a few minutes to greet one another and re-connect as colleagues and collaborative learners. Follow up on any issues left over from the previous group meeting and then proceed to address the following:

2.5 Discuss with your colleagues your most significant reactions to the material and independent learning exercises presented in this chapter. In particular, share your thoughts and feelings about the idea of multiple intelligences, the significance and implications of emotional intelligence, the relevance of psychological type theory, and perspectives on learning styles.

2.6 Share with your colleagues what you have discovered about yourself as a learner. Then discuss how you plan to use that self-awareness to enhance your psychosocial functioning as a student and independent learner, a member of a collaborative learning group, and later as a professional social worker and a lifelong learner.

Portfolio Exercise

2.7 Following the independent and collaborative group learning exercises, prepare a one- to two-page word-processed essay (300–500 words) in which you summarize your understanding of yourself as a learner for social work. Refer to your responses to the independent and collaborative group exercises as you thoughtfully explore your multiple intelligences, emotional intelligence, psychological type, and learning style preferences. Discuss what you have discovered about your strengths and weaknesses as a learner. Following that, describe specifically how you might plan to grow and develop as an active, self-directed, and collaborative learner during your university studies and throughout your professional social work career.

Determining Your Social Work Learning Needs

Contemporary social workers must be more knowledgeable, more ethical, more skillful, and more effective in providing professional service than ever before. There are numerous reasons for these heightened expectations. Demands for greater accountability, improved outcomes, and better efficiency represent just a few. Perhaps the most important factors, however, involve our moral obligations as human beings and our ethical principles as professional social workers. *The Code of Ethics of the National Association of Social Workers* requires social workers to "develop and enhance their professional expertise . . . [and] . . . continually strive to increase their professional knowledge and skills and to apply them in practice" (National Association of Social Workers, 1999, p. 6).

A comprehensive knowledge base, adherence to a value-based code of ethics, and advanced expertise are, of course, fundamental requisites for professional status. As potential consumers, we expect professionals, especially those whose decisions and actions affect the lives of vulnerable persons, to be knowledgeable, ethical, and expert in their service. Indeed, we rely on social workers to possess both general knowledge and specialized, advanced levels of expertise in one or more areas of service. We depend on professional social workers to read, study, and learn about recent advances in pertinent knowledge and then to apply this knowledge in their efforts to serve others.

In this chapter, we discuss the dimensions of the general social work knowledge base and review the major sources of that professional foundation (see Box 3.1). We encourage you to collect and consider documentary evidence of prior learning to aid in the assessment process and for use in your social work portfolio. We request that you conduct a thorough assessment of your current proficiency in the knowledge base and then, based on your self-assessment, identify your social work learning needs.

The Social Work Knowledge Base

The elements of the general social work knowledge base are derived from several sources. Certainly, the Council on Social Work Education (CSWE), the National Association of Social Workers (NASW), university accreditation organizations, consumer and advocacy groups, and other stakeholders and constituents influence the nature and scope of the knowledge base. Legislation enacted by state and national governments and the results of relevant court cases also have considerable impact. The knowledge base, of course, changes over time to reflect the evolving nature and scope of the profession as well as advances in theoretical innovations, empirical research findings, and changes in policy.

The Council on Social Work Education serves as the accrediting body for schools and departments of social work in the United States. CSWE identifies the areas of knowledge, values, and skills that all B.S.W. and M.S.W. students should address during their programs of study. These

BOX

3.1   **CHAPTER PURPOSES**

The primary purposes of this chapter are to familiarize you with the dimensions of the general social work knowledge base, help you to identify and collect relevant documents for your social work portfolio, enable you to assess your current level of knowledge proficiency, and help you to identify your social work learning needs.

Goals

Following completion of this chapter, you should be able to:

- Describe and discuss the general dimensions of the social work knowledge base
- Gather documents for inclusion in your social work portfolio
- Assess and discuss your current proficiency in the general social work knowledge base
- Identify your current social work learning needs

are described in the *Curriculum Policy Statement* (Council on Social Work Education, 1992), the *Handbook of Accreditation Standards and Procedures* (Council on Social Work Education, 1994), and the proposed *Educational Policy and Accreditation Standards (EPAS)* (Council on Social Work Education, 2001). For example, CSWE expects students from accredited social work programs to address content from the following curriculum areas: social work values and ethics, diversity, populations at risk, social and economic justice, human behavior and the social environment, social welfare policy and services, social work practice, research, and practicum.

The recently proposed CSWE *Educational Policy and Accreditation Standards (EPAS)* will, undoubtedly, have a substantial impact on the scope of the general social work knowledge base. In the preamble to the *EPAS*, the council describes the profession in this fashion:

> Social work promotes human well-being by strengthening opportunities, resources, and capacities of people in their environments and by creating policies and services to correct conditions that limit human rights and the quality of life. The social work profession works to eliminate poverty, discrimination, and oppression. Guided by a person-in-environment perspective and respect for human diversity, the profession works to effect social and economic justice worldwide. (Council on Social Work Education, 2001)

The council elaborates on the description of social work by outlining the profession's major purposes:

> The social work profession receives its sanction from public and private auspices and is the primary profession in the development, provision, and evaluation of social services. Professional social workers are leaders in a variety of organizational settings and service delivery systems within a global context.
>
> The profession of social work is based on the values of service, social and economic justice, dignity and worth of the person, importance of human relationships, and integrity and competence in practice. With these values as defining principles, the purposes of social work are:
>
> - To enhance human well-being and alleviate poverty, oppression, and other forms of social injustice.
> - To enhance the social functioning and interactions of individuals, families, groups, organizations, communities, and society by involving them in accomplishing goals, developing resources, and preventing and alleviating distress.
> - To formulate and implement social policies, services, and programs that meet basic human needs and support the development of human capacities.

- To pursue policies, services, and resources through advocacy and social or political actions to promote social and economic justice.
- To develop and use research, knowledge, and skills that advance social work practice.
- To develop and apply practice in the context of diverse cultures. (Council on Social Work Education, 2001)

The nature and purposes of the social work profession are, of course, reflected within the general knowledge base. As a helping profession, intellectual, academic, or scientific knowledge alone, however, is wholly insufficient. Values and skills are also needed. These dimensions are also included within the social work knowledge base.

Within the area of values and ethics, for example, the Council on Social Work Education indicates that:

> The educational experience provides students with the opportunity to be aware of personal values; develop, demonstrate and promote the values of the profession; and analyze ethical dilemmas and the ways in which these dilemmas affect the quality of services. (Council on Social Work Education, 2001)

The council suggests that social work educational programs include information about values and ethical decision making as published in the *Code of Ethics of the National Association of Social Workers*. In the Code of Ethics, NASW identifies several core social work values. An ethical principle is derived from each of these core values to guide the decisions and actions of professional social workers. The core values and their associated ethical principles include:

Value: *Service*
Ethical Principle: *Social workers' primary goal is to help people in need and to address social problems.*
Social workers elevate service to others above self-interest. Social workers draw on their knowledge, values, and skills to help people in need and to address social problems. Social workers are encouraged to volunteer some portion of their professional skills with no expectation of significant financial return (pro bono service).

Value: *Social Justice*
Ethical Principle: *Social workers challenge social injustice.*
Social workers pursue social change, particularly with and on behalf of vulnerable and oppressed individuals and groups of people. Social workers' social change efforts are focused primarily on issues of poverty, unemployment, discrimination, and other forms of social injustice. These activities seek to promote sensitivity to and knowledge about oppression and cultural and ethnic diversity. Social workers strive to ensure access to needed information, services, and resources; equality of opportunity; and meaningful participation in decision making for all people.

Value: *Dignity and Worth of the Person*
Ethical Principle: *Social workers respect the inherent dignity and worth of the person.*
Social workers treat each person in a caring and respectful fashion, mindful of individual differences and cultural and ethnic diversity. Social workers promote clients' socially responsible self-determination. Social workers seek to enhance clients' capacity and opportunity to change and to address their own needs. Social workers are cognizant of their dual responsibility to clients and to the broader society. They seek to resolve conflicts between clients' interests and the broader society's interests in a socially responsible manner consistent with the values, ethical principles, and ethical standards of the profession.

Value: *Importance of Human Relationships*
Ethical Principle: *Social workers recognize the central importance of human relationships.*
Social workers understand that relationships between and among people are an important vehicle for change. Social workers engage people as partners in the helping process. Social workers seek to strengthen relationships among people in a purposeful effort to promote, restore, maintain, and enhance the well being of individuals, families, social groups, organizations, and communities.

Value: *Integrity*
Ethical Principle: *Social workers behave in a trustworthy manner.*
Social workers are continually aware of the profession's mission, values, ethical principles, and ethical standards and practice in a manner consistent with them. Social workers act honestly and responsibly and promote ethical practices on the part of the organizations with which they are affiliated.

Value: *Competence*
Ethical Principle: *Social workers practice within their areas of competence and develop and enhance their professional expertise.*
Social workers continually strive to increase their professional knowledge and skills and to apply them in practice. Social workers should aspire to contribute to the knowledge base of the profession. (National Association of Social Workers, 1999, pp. 5–6)

In a helping profession, knowledge and values would be of limited utility unless they were applied in the form of skills and abilities. There are numerous sources of information about the skills that social workers need to demonstrate in their service activities. For example, the Council on Social Work Education requires accredited schools and departments of social work to prepare social workers to:

- Apply critical thinking skills within the context of professional social work practice.
- Engage in ethical decision making within the values of the social work profession.
- Practice without discrimination and with respect, knowledge, and skills related to clients' age, culture, class, disability, ethnicity, family structure, gender, national origin, race, religion, and sexual orientation.
- Understand the forms and mechanisms of oppression and discrimination and apply strategies of advocacy and social change that advance social and economic justice.
- Understand and interpret the history of the social work profession and its current structures and issues.
- Apply the knowledge and skills of social work practice with systems of all sizes.
- Use theoretical frameworks to understand individual development and behavior and the interactions among individuals and between individuals and families, groups, organizations, and communities.
- Analyze, formulate, and influence social policies.
- Evaluate research studies and apply findings to practice, and evaluate their own practice interventions.
- Use communication skills differentially across client populations, colleagues, and communities.
- Use supervision and consultation appropriate to social work practice.
- Function within the structure of organizations and service delivery systems, and seek necessary organizational change. (Council on Social Work Education, 2001)

More than 20 years ago, the National Association of Social Workers outlined several basic skills or abilities that all social workers should master. These included the ability to:

- Listen to others with understanding and purpose.
- Elicit information and assemble relevant facts to prepare a social history, assessment, and report.
- Create and maintain professional helping relationships.
- Observe and interpret verbal and nonverbal behavior and use knowledge of personality theory and diagnostic methods.

- Engage clients (including individuals, families, groups, and communities) in efforts to re-solve their own problems and to gain trust.
- Discuss sensitive emotional subjects supportively and without being threatening.
- Create innovative solutions to clients' needs.
- Determine the need to terminate the therapeutic relationship.
- Conduct research, or interpret the findings of research and professional literature.
- Mediate and negotiate between conflicting parties.
- Provide inter-organizational liaison services.
- Interpret and communicate social needs to funding sources, the public, or legislators. (National Association of Social Workers, 1981, pp. 17–18)

These skills and abilities remain relevant today, although several would need to be updated to reflect the changing nature of the society and service contexts. Cournoyer (2000) has also inte-grated several fundamental abilities within *The Social Work Skills Workbook*. He identified more than 50 discrete social work skills within the areas of ethical decision making, basic talking and lis-tening, and those that relate to each of seven common phases or processes of service: preparing, beginning, exploring, assessing, contracting, working and evaluating, and ending.

The General Social Work Knowledge Base

The factors just described tend to be reflected in the nationally standardized social work licens-ing examinations used throughout the United States. Construction of the examinations is spon-sored and overseen by the Association of Social Work Boards (ASWB). ASWB is composed of representatives from the state organizations (e.g., agencies, boards, or bureaus) charged with the legal regulation and oversight of the social work profession. The nationally standardized exami-nation items are regularly updated to match the requirements of contemporary social work as de-termined by scientifically designed and conducted research studies of practicing professionals.

The association uses Bloom's Cognitive Taxonomy (Bloom & Krathwohl, 1956) as a concep-tual framework for the organization and composition of examination items. Persons who take the social work certification or licensing examinations are expected to demonstrate that they can:

- *Remember* relevant social work material (e.g., recall facts and theoretical concepts).
- *Understand* the meaning and relevance of social work material (e.g., comprehend, interpret, explain, and summarize).
- *Apply* the social work material accurately in a professional situation (e.g., employ rules, methods, principles, and concepts in social work contexts).
- *Analyze* the elements of the material (e.g., identify the relationships and organizational structure of various knowledge components relevant to the item).
- *Synthesize* components of recalled information to adapt, form, or create a new organiza-tional structure or system.
- *Evaluate* the relevance and relative value of information for a defined purpose.

The first four dimensions are prominent throughout the basic and intermediate level social work examinations whereas all six are reflected in the advanced and clinical versions. Of course, all of these cognitive abilities (i.e., remembering, understanding, applying, analyzing, synthesiz-ing, and evaluating) are essential for the sophisticated critical thinking needed by advanced help-ing professionals.

The specific requirements for social work licensure or certification vary somewhat from state to state.[1] In general, however, states that regulate the profession and practice of social work tend to establish two to four levels or categories of social worker. The term certified or licensed social worker (CSW or LSW) often refers to the first level. Some states require bachelor of social work (B.S.W.) graduates to take an examination immediately following receipt of their degree. The ASWB-sponsored basic examination is commonly used for that purpose. Other states require master of social work (M.S.W.) graduates to take the intermediate examination. The advanced and clinical examinations tend to be used to qualify higher levels of practitioner and follow 2 or more years of supervised social work practice experience. The term certified or licensed clinical social worker (CCSW or LCSW) commonly refers to a higher level of state credential.

As described by ASWB (2000), the basic examination addresses 11 major content areas. These domains reflect the scope of the general social work knowledge base (see Box 3.2). (Percentages indicate the proportion of exam items classified within a content area.)

All social workers may be expected to demonstrate proficiency in the knowledge, values, and skills reflected in these domains. You could learn a great deal about your general readiness for professional service simply by asking yourself, "How well do I know and how expertly can I apply the knowledge, values, and abilities identified by CSWE, NASW, and ASWB?" You might discover even more about your proficiency in the general social work knowledge base by collecting and examining several pertinent documents. These documents may be included within your social work portfolio. Indeed, the portfolio can serve as an important resource for assessing social work knowledge, values, and expertise.

Social workers tend to view human experience from ecological and holistic perspectives. We usually consider multiple dimensions in our efforts to understand and serve others. We encourage you to approach assessment of your current social work knowledge and expertise in a similar fashion, drawing on as many different sources of information as possible.

One of the first steps in any assessment process is the identification, location, and collection of information related to the topic in question. Much of what you might collect for the purpose of assessing your general social work knowledge could also be incorporated within a social work portfolio. Among other materials, we suggest that you collect certificates, diplomas, and professional licenses; academic transcripts; course syllabi and workshop flyers or brochures; learning products (e.g., written papers, essays, examinations); performance appraisals; and letters of reference or recommendation.

Certificates, Licenses, and Diplomas

Certificates, licenses, and diplomas serve to document attainment of some status and, we sincerely hope, some degree of learning. They are typically awarded following completion of a program of study or upon demonstration of a certain level of competence or proficiency. Indeed, they "certify" that a person deserves the designated status. Such documents range in value or importance. For example, most people view a "certificate of attendance" as less significant that either

---

[1] Most U.S. states, the District of Columbia, and the Virgin Islands use one or more of the nationally standardized examinations sponsored and developed by the Association of Social Work Boards (ASWB). You may review information about ASWB-sponsored examinations online at www.aswb.org. California licenses clinical social workers only and sponsored the creation of a different examination. For online access to the California Board of Behavioral Sciences go to www.bbs.ca.gov. Michigan and Puerto Rico do not require applicants to complete an examination for social work licensure or certification.

Content Area	Percentage of Items
I. Human Development and Behavior	15%
A. Theoretical approaches to understanding individuals, families, groups, communities, and organizations	
B. Human growth and development	
C. Human behavior in the social environment	
D. Impact of crises and changes	
E. Abnormal and addictive behaviors	
F. Dynamics of abuse and neglect	
II. Effects of Diversity	7%
III. Assessment in Social Work Practice	23%
A. Social history and collateral data	
B. Use of assessment instruments	
C. Problem identification	
D. Effects of the environment on client behavior	
E. Assessment of client strengths and weaknesses	
F. Assessment of mental and behavioral disorders	
G. Indicators of abuse and neglect	
H. Indicators of danger to self and others	
IV. Social Work Practice with Individuals, Couples, Families, Groups, and Communities	23%
A. Theoretical approaches and models of practice	
B. The intervention process	
C. Components of the intervention process	
D. Matching intervention with client needs	
E. Intervention techniques	
F. Intervention with couples, families, and groups	
G. Intervention with communities	
H. Professional use of self	
I. Use of collaborative relationships in social work practice	
V. Interpersonal Communication	7%
A. Theories and principles of communication	
B. Techniques of communicating	
VI. Professional Social Worker/Client Relationship	4%
A. Relationship concepts	
B. Relationship practice	
VII. Professional Values and Ethics	7%
A. Responsibility to the client	
B. Responsibility to the profession	
C. Confidentiality	
D. Self-determination	
VIII. Supervision in Social Work	3%
A. Educational functions of supervision	
B. Administrative functions of supervision	
IX. Practice Evaluation and the Utilization of Research	3%
A. Methods of data collection	
B. Research design and data analysis	
X. Service Delivery	7%
A. Client rights and entitlements	
B. Implementation of organizational policies and procedures	
XI. Social Work Administration	3%
A. Staffing and human resource management	
B. Social work program management	

a diploma from a prestigious university or a state license that authorizes one to engage in the professional practice of social work. All such documents, however, provide tangible evidence of learning activities.

Academic Transcripts

Academic transcripts represent a rich source of information about a person's formal learning history. Transcripts typically include letter or numerical grades or some other general indicator of performance (e.g., pass/fail or satisfactory/unsatisfactory). They also commonly report course withdrawals and those repeated for a better grade.

Trends of various kinds may also be revealed. For example, a person may enjoy literature. Her transcript indicates that she took many more such courses than required for graduation and generally performed extremely well in them. She earned grades of A or A– in every one of her literature classes. However, the same transcript suggests that she did less well in science courses. She took the bare minimum required and earned grades of C and D.

Academic transcripts may also reflect growth and progress over time. For example, it is quite common for people to struggle during the early portions of their studies but then demonstrate marked improvement during the latter part. Sometimes this progress is related to the selection of a major, when students begin to take more courses that they genuinely prefer.

Course Syllabi

Academic transcripts and course grades provide a great deal of information about the general nature of your educational pursuits and performance. However, because they are commonly limited to course numbers and titles, credit hours, and grades, the actual material addressed in courses remains unknown. Course syllabi often provide more detailed information regarding the content and learning experience. Syllabi usually contain a course description, learning objectives, polices and grading guidelines, reading requirements, assignments, and projects.

Both classroom and field practicum course syllabi contain useful data. So do the brochures, flyers, and bulletins that accompany professional workshops, institutes, seminars, and conferences. They are similar to course syllabi in this regard.

Learning Products

Assorted written documents such as research papers, essays, examinations, and reports of various kinds are frequently prepared for classroom or field practicum courses. Some high schools and colleges require senior projects, some graduate programs expect students to complete master's theses, and of course, dissertations are required for most doctoral degrees. You might complete a final examination for one course, prepare a major paper for another, write an essay for a third, present a poster session in a fourth, and deliver an oral presentation and slide show in a fifth. In some courses, you might videotape or audiotape interviews with a simulated client. In many practicum settings, students are expected to prepare process recordings and summary self-evaluations of their service to clients.

You may produce a report, a manual, or a monograph for a social service related job or as part of a volunteer activity. You might even write an article for a magazine or journal or a chapter of a book. We refer to these materials and documents as learning products. They range all the way from lecture notes to major papers and reports that you formally prepare for a course, academic program, or job.

Learning products are ideal for the purposes of assessment. They represent extraordinarily valuable evidence of learning and, importantly, may be among the most vital components of a social work portfolio.

Performance Appraisals, Evaluations, and Feedback

At various points during their academic studies, students commonly receive various forms of written evaluation and feedback that go beyond numerical scores, letter grades, or diplomas. Employees often undergo performance reviews, and volunteers are sometimes provided with written feedback about their service as well.

For example, a professor may provide written feedback concerning a paper you submit for a course. You might receive a formal evaluation as part of your field practicum experience. Supervisors from social service related job or volunteer experiences might prepare performance appraisals or perhaps write letters of recommendation. Forms of evaluation and feedback regarding aspects of your social work knowledge, values, expertise, and performance serve as documentary evidence for assessment. They often contribute immeasurably to self-understanding, and of course, they may also add a valuable dimension to a social work portfolio.

Exercises

In this chapter, you learned about the general professional knowledge, values, and expertise needed by all social workers. You also became familiar with several documents that may be used for assessment, as evidence of learning, and for incorporation within your social work portfolio. Indeed, you considered numerous materials related to various learning experiences.

From exercises in earlier chapters, you also have written several paragraphs, notes, and short essays. You have completed other exercises to enhance your self-understanding as a lifelong learner. The following exercises build on earlier activities by helping you assess your proficiency in the general social work knowledge base and identify your learning needs. They will also contribute a great deal to the development of your social work portfolio.

Independent Learning Exercises

3.1 Please collect certificates, diplomas, licenses, academic transcripts, course syllabi, workshop flyers, seminar brochures, written products that resulted from learning experiences, and various forms of evaluation, performance appraisal, and feedback you have received. Include letters of reference or recommendation. Now organize these materials into different folders: one for certificates, diplomas, awards, licenses, and academic transcripts; a second for course syllabi and workshop or seminar brochures; a third for learning products; and a fourth for performance appraisals, evaluative feedback, and letters of reference or recommendation. You might also have a folder for printed versions of your responses to learning exercises from this book. Label each folder and then organize dated documents within each folder in reverse chronological order—where the most recent materials are on top and the oldest are on the bottom.

3.2 Examine the folder that contains your academic transcripts, certificates, awards, diplomas, and licenses. Review these materials from the earliest to most recent. Include the transcript from your current program of study, even though it is incomplete.

As you review the materials, reflect upon what they might suggest about your interests, talents, and abilities. What do they indicate about areas of weakness or disinterest? What subjects have been emphasized? Which pertinent subjects are not represented? What do they reveal about your readiness for a career as a social work professional? Summarize your impressions, reactions, and conclusions in a short word-processed essay of two or three paragraphs.

3.3 Turn to the folder that contains course syllabi and workshop brochures. Look closely at explicit or implicit learning objectives of the various courses, seminars, and workshops. Reflect upon what you learned from the experiences and consider what more you would like to learn about these topics. Following your reflection, prepare a short word-processed essay about the overall impact of these learning experiences on your growth and development as a social worker.

3.4 Examine the contents of the folder that includes various learning products of various kinds along with the one that contains documents that refer to your performance and abilities (e.g., appraisals or evaluations, letters of reference). Please review these documents in considerable depth. Carefully read each learning product and evaluation. Begin with the earliest and continue on to the most recent. Following your review, prepare a brief word-processed response (a paragraph or so) to the following questions:

a. Taken as a whole, do the documents appear to reflect a progression toward higher quality and greater professional sophistication? In general, are more recent learning products superior to earlier ones?

b. What do the learning products, performance evaluations, and letters of reference suggest about your ability to think critically and to apply, analyze, synthesize, and evaluate (i.e., the higher levels of Bloom's Cognitive Taxonomy)?

c. What do the documents indicate about your energy or passion and commitment for core social work values?

d. What do the materials suggest about your integration of social work knowledge, values, and expertise within an emerging professional philosophy, perspective, or approach?

e. Which of the principles of learning (e.g., humility; empathy; fairness; courage; honesty and integrity; clarity, accuracy, and precision; relevance; intellectual sophistication; and logic) are clearly evident within the learning products or reflected by the evaluations and letters of reference? Which are not?

Now, with your responses to these questions in mind, word process a brief assessment of each of your major learning products (e.g., essays, reports, and papers). The written assessment of each significant learning product is central to a high-quality portfolio.

Following the preparation of the individual assessments, word process a one- to two-page essay in which you summarize and reflect upon the performance evaluations or appraisals and letters of reference you have received.

3.5 Go to Appendix 4 and complete the Self-Assessment of Social Work Knowledge Survey. Review and reflect upon your responses to the instrument. Then word process a paragraph or so in response to each of the following questions:

a. What do your responses to the survey suggest about your proficiency in the general social work knowledge base?

    b. In what areas do you tend to reflect the greatest proficiency and in which do you seem to reflect the weakest?

    c. What do your responses indicate about your current social work learning needs?

3.6 Incorporate your responses to the earlier questions as you prepare a word-processed, two- to five-page essay entitled, "Summary Self-Assessment of Social Work Knowledge." Consider both your assessment of the documents for your portfolio as well as your responses to the Social Work Knowledge Survey. Be sure to identify and describe what you need to learn to be prepared for competent professional social work practice during the early portion of the 21st century.

Collaborative Group Learning Exercises

3.7 In your group, share your reactions to all the work necessary to assemble the documentation and complete the independent learning exercises. Discuss which aspects you found useful or enlightening as well as those you thought were nonproductive or irrelevant.

3.8 Along with your colleagues, consider the social work knowledge, values, skills, and abilities expected by the Council on Social Work Education, the National Association of Social Workers, and the Association of Social Work Boards in its nationally standardized social work licensing examinations. Considering the rapid nature of change within contemporary society, what else do you think social workers should learn that is not suggested by these outlines? Discuss your rationale for this additional learning. Also discuss among yourselves those content areas that you need to study to perform well on the ASWB-sponsored licensing exams. Share with one another how you plan to further your learning in these areas.

Portfolio Exercise

At this point, you have a substantial collection of materials organized into different folders. You have also completed several written exercises. Importantly, you have a self-assessment to accompany each of your major learning products. You also have a substantial essay entitled, "Summary Self-Assessment of Social Work Knowledge." Nonetheless, you are still very much in the preliminary stages of developing your social work portfolio and using it to plan, assess, and document your lifelong learning.

3.9 Refer to Table 3.1 to help you organize the kinds of documentary evidence that you have thus far collected. Use your word-processing computer program to create a table that contains the eight columns and about ten rows. Indicate within each cell wherever you have documentary evidence of learning. Place a check mark within the cell that best corresponds to the form of evidence. We have used the first column within the Forms of Documentary Evidence category to recognize Learning Products. We believe that learning products represent the best evidence of learning, especially when they are accompanied by a corresponding self-assessment. As you recall, learning products are those documents that you have created as part of some learning activity. Essays, examinations, papers, articles, or reports that you have written are examples of common learning products. You might also have an audio- or videotape or even a computerized presentation such as a slide show that you have prepared. Learning products are your own creations. The work of other people, of course, would not be included.

TABLE 3.1   DOCUMENTARY EVIDENCE OF LEARNING

Forms of Documentary Evidence

Social Work Content Area	Learning Product (e.g., Paper, Report)	Self-Assessment of Learning Product	Course, Seminar, or Workshop Syllabi or Transcript	Performance Evaluation or Letter of Reference	Award, Certificate, License	Other
1 Social Work Values & Ethics						
2 Diversity						
3 Populations-at-Risk and Social & Economic Justice						
4 Human Behavior & Social Environment						
5 Social Welfare Policy & Services						
6 Social Work Practice						
7 Research						
8 Field Practicum						
Totals						

Following your classification of the various forms of documentary evidence, please consider the overall quality of the evidence. Identify those categories where you have substantial evidence of learning and those where you have limited evidence. Ideally, there should be at least one high-quality learning product and a corresponding self-assessment for each of the eight social work content areas.

Exploring a Social Work Career and Preparing a Résumé

The range of possible career paths within the profession of social work is incredibly broad and diverse. You could not conceivably pursue all of them. We imagine, however, that as a social work student you have at least a beginning vision of a successful professional career and perhaps even some notion of what would be your ideal social work position.

In this chapter (see Box 4.1), we hope to engage you in the fundamental steps of exploring a career in social work and preparing a draft version of a professional résumé. In undertaking such a process, however, we recognize that career planning is as much art as science and that it is never truly complete. Most social workers do not discover a "perfect" job that remains so throughout their entire professional career. Indeed, you are quite likely to have eight, ten, or more different positions during your lifetime of service as a social worker. Through the material and exercises presented in this chapter, we hope that you begin to formulate a career path and identify your ideal social work position.

We hope that you become familiar with the career exploration and planning process so that if and when you find it necessary or desirable to change the nature and course of your social work service, you may readily undertake the process again in the future. Before looking ahead, however, we would like you to reflect upon your personality characteristics as they relate to occupational choice.

Personality Characteristics and Occupational Choice

John L. Holland observed that people reflect their personality characteristics in the process of career selection (1985a; 1997). Author of *The Self-Directed Search* (*SDS*), an instrument that helps identify personality dimensions associated with career choice, Holland identified the following personal orientations: *realistic, investigative, artistic, social, enterprising,* and *conventional* (1985b; Holland, Powell, & Fritzsche, 1994):

- *Realistic (R)*: Realistic individuals tend be practical, authentic, humble, and pragmatic. They often enjoy working with their hands, operating machines, or using tools. They frequently reflect considerable mechanical and athletic ability. Realistic persons might be found working as mechanics, electricians, ranchers, carpenters, technicians, and surveyors.
- *Investigative (I)*: Investigative individuals tend to reflect aptitudes within the areas of science and mathematics. They are often curious, rational, objective, analytic, and intellectual. They frequently like to work alone. They often enjoy problem-solving activities and like to understand how and why things occur. Investigative people are often found working as physicists, biologists, chemists, geologists, scientists, and advanced technicians.
- *Artistic (A)*: Artistic people tend to be open, creative, imaginative, innovative, independent, and idealistic. They tend to enjoy music, art, and literature. In general, artistic persons enjoy

CHAPTER PURPOSES

The purposes of this chapter are to introduce you to the processes of social work career exploration and planning, consider your personality characteristics in relation to occupational choice, prepare a career time-line, help you to develop a professional résumé, and assist you to identify an ideal social work position.

Goals

Following completion of this chapter, you should be able to:

- Identify and discuss your personality orientations and occupational profile
- Prepare and discuss your career timeline
- Prepare a preliminary résumé for inclusion in your social work portfolio
- Describe a professional career path and ideal social work position

---

creating original works or products. Artistic persons may be found working as musicians, writers, painters, sculptors, actors, or directors.
- *Social (S)*: Social people tend to be understanding, compassionate, warm, sociable, and friendly. They usually like being around other people. They prefer cooperation to competition. Social people are often found working as social workers, teachers, counselors, psychologists, therapists of various kinds, or members of the clergy.
- *Enterprising (E)*: Enterprising people tend to be outgoing, confident, ambitious, and risk taking. They often enjoy positions of leadership or authority, like to speak in public, and are comfortable with responsibility. Enterprising individuals may be found working as managers, lawyers, executives, promoters, or salespeople.
- *Conventional (C)*: Conventional persons tend to be responsible, dependable, hardworking, and organized. They often enjoy planning and organizing things and events. Conventional people might be found working as financial consultants, bankers, brokers, tax advisers, or accountants.

Results from the Self-Directed Search are typically reported as three letters, according to the three most highly rated dimensions. For example, a person's profile might be presented as RIA (realistic, investigative, artistic)—where *R* represents the most highly rated dimension, *I* the next, and *A* the third most highly rated of Holland's six RIASEC personality groupings.

As indicated earlier, people interested in social work often possess dominant strength in the social dimension. More specifically, many social workers tend to reflect an SEC occupational profile (social, enterprising, and conventional). This makes a good deal of sense. According to Holland, such individuals like to be with and help others, are outgoing and comfortable with leadership and responsibility, and enjoy planning and organizing activities or interventions required to provide social services in contemporary society. Of course, many wonderful social workers reflect other occupational profiles and tend to feel most comfortable when their personality profiles match the kind and nature of social work they perform.

As a social work student, you probably already know just how vast is the array of potential career pathways within the field of social work. You might be interested in many areas. However, if you aspire to be a truly successful social worker, you must narrow your focus to those few paths that represent a good fit with your own personality, values, interests, talents, and abilities. Establishing a general career direction can help provide focus during your academic program and immediately following graduation, and it may be useful when you change careers or return to the work force after a prolonged absence. In a real sense, career planning is an ongoing process that is just as continuous as lifelong learning.

Effective career planning requires a great deal of self-understanding about your knowledge, skills and abilities, aptitudes, personality, interests, and values. Most colleges and universities have career placement centers that contain resources for undertaking a comprehensive vocational assessment. These centers usually have access to various tests, inventories, questionnaires, and surveys that aid in assessment and planning. In addition to the Self-Directed Search,[1] the Career Key[2] is a well-known instrument based on the original work of John L. Holland. Other widely used instruments for the assessment of vocational aptitudes and interests are the General Aptitude Test Battery, Strong-Campbell Interest Inventory, the Campbell Interest and Skill Survey (CISS),[3] the Differential Aptitude Test, and the Minnesota Vocational Interest Inventory.

Personality tests of various kinds, including the Myers-Briggs Type Indicator (MBTI), the Keirsey Temperament Sorter, and the Sixteen Personality Factor Questionnaire[4] may help determine how your personal characteristics match those of people in various occupations and professions. Although the scores and profiles reflected on these measures should never be used exclusively to determine a specific career to follow, they may be of considerable assistance in helping you narrow the range of choices and establish a general direction.

In addition to personality, interests, and aptitudes, lifestyle preferences also play significant roles in career planning. If you choose a career or a position that differs markedly from or conflicts with your beliefs, expectations, and your social and economic needs, you may anticipate a good deal of dissatisfaction and distress. These factors become significant as you explore various careers within the field of social work. Be sure to consider how your preferences might change in the future. For example, you may now be single, without children or extensive family responsibilities, and would be quite comfortable with lots of "on-call" emergency work. You might enjoy serving people at short notice in emergency or crisis situations. You might also like to travel frequently as part of your work. Later on, however, you might have children in school or be responsible for the care of an elderly parent and prefer to engage in work that involves a predictable schedule with little crisis work and infrequent travel.

The process of career selection usually extends over a number of years. It often begins during late childhood and continues into adulthood. Understandably, personal values, attitudes, dreams, and aspirations influence career choices. As a social work student, you are already considering a professional identity. You think you want to be a social worker—or at least to earn a social work degree. Quite a few students seek social work degrees but prefer to view themselves

---

[1] The Self-Directed Search is available online at www.self-directed-search.com/index.html. To receive the report based on your answers, you must pay a small fee by credit card.

[2] The Career Key is available online at www.ncsu.edu/careerkey/. You may complete the instrument and receive the results free of charge.

[3] You may locate the Campbell Interest and Skill Survey (CISS) online at the U.S. News Career Search Site at www.usnews.com/usnews/edu/careers/ccciss.htm. To receive a 12-page personalized career planning and action report based on your responses, you must mail the completed survey along with a small fee to the address listed on the form.

[4] The ERIC Clearinghouse on Assessment, Evaluation, and Research contains a wealth of information about various tests and instruments. You may access their Web site at www.ericae.net.

as something else (e.g., counselor, psychotherapist, administrator, planner). The field of social work is often highly attractive precisely because it offers such a variety of career opportunities in many different types of work environments. A wide array of positions and job functions are possible for social work graduates. Indeed, social work may encompass the widest range of diverse positions and service opportunities of all the professions.

Social workers are commonly employed in numerous organizational or institutional areas in the private nonprofit as well as the private for-profit sectors and within the federal, state, local, and military dimensions of the public sector. Social workers serve in the fields of aging, child and family welfare, child and family services, criminal justice, health, mental health and substance misuse, occupational services, employment assistance programs, school systems, vocational services, and numerous other contexts.[5]

Social workers address an incredibly vast number of social problems in their service to others. Increasingly, social workers serve prevention as well as intervention functions in their efforts to help persons affected by poverty, unemployment, homelessness; spouse, child, and elder abuse; sexual abuse of children and dependent persons; mental illness; physical illness and disability; alcohol and drug use and abuse; discrimination on the basis of age, gender, race, ethnicity, religion, physical ability, sexual orientation, and other forms of social injustice; sexual offenses such as rape and molestation; and a host of social issues associated with immigration, changing societal demographics, and the technological and information revolution (Gibelman, 1995).

Community attempts to address social problems and issues have led to the development of agencies, organizations, and programs within both the private and public sectors. Although an increasing number of social workers pursue careers as independent self-employed practitioners, most tend to be employed within organizational contexts. As a part of its lengthy description of social work, the United States Bureau of Labor Statistics (BLS)[6] provides the following job descriptions:

- *Clinical social workers* offer psychotherapy or counseling and a range of diagnostic services in public agencies, clinics, and private practice.
- *Child welfare or family services social workers* may counsel children and youths who have difficulty adjusting socially, advise parents on how to care for disabled children, or arrange for homemaker services during a parent's illness. If children have serious problems in school, child welfare workers may consult with parents, teachers, and counselors to identify underlying causes and develop plans for treatment. Some social workers assist single parents, arrange adoptions, and help find foster homes for neglected, abandoned, or abused children. Child welfare workers also work in residential institutions for children and adolescents.
- *Child or adult protective services social workers* investigate reports of abuse and neglect and intervene if necessary. They may initiate legal action to remove children from homes and place them temporarily in an emergency shelter or with a foster family.
- *Mental health social workers* provide services for persons with mental or emotional problems. Such services include individual and group therapy, outreach, crisis intervention, social rehabilitation, and training in skills of everyday living. They may also help plan for supportive services to ease patients' return to the community.

---

[5] For information about several social work careers, visit the Social Work Careers section of the National Association of Social Workers (NASW) Web site at www.socialworkers.org/practice/career.htm.

[6] Access the Social Worker section of the Bureau of Labor Statistics, U.S. Department of Labor, *Occupational Outlook Handbook*, 2000–01 Edition, online at stats.bls.gov/oco/ocos060.htm.

- *Health care social workers* help patients and their families cope with chronic, acute, or terminal illnesses and handle problems that may stand in the way of recovery or rehabilitation. They may organize support groups for families of patients suffering from cancer, AIDS, Alzheimer's disease, or other illnesses. They also advise family caregivers, counsel patients, and help plan for their needs after discharge by arranging for at-home services—from meals-on-wheels to oxygen equipment. Some work on interdisciplinary teams that evaluate certain kinds of patients—geriatric or organ transplant patients, for example.
- *School social workers* diagnose students' problems and arrange needed services, counsel children in trouble, and help integrate disabled students into the general school population. School social workers deal with problems such as student pregnancy, misbehavior in class, and excessive absences. They also advise teachers on how to cope with problem students.
- *Criminal justice social workers* make recommendations to courts, prepare pre-sentencing assessments, and provide services to prison inmates and their families. Probation and parole officers provide similar services to individuals sentenced by a court to parole or probation.
- *Occupational social workers* usually work in a corporation's personnel department or health unit. Through employee assistance programs, they help workers cope with job-related pressures or personal problems that affect the quality of their work. They often offer direct counseling to employees whose performance is hindered by emotional or family problems or substance abuse. They also develop education programs and refer workers to specialized community programs.
- *Gerontology social workers* specialize in services to the aged. They run support groups for family caregivers or for the adult children of aging parents. Also, they advise elderly people or family members about the choices in such areas as housing, transportation, and long-term care; they also coordinate and monitor services.
- *Social work administrators* perform overall management tasks in a hospital, clinic, or other setting that offers social worker services.
- *Social work planners and policy-makers* develop programs to address such issues as child abuse, homelessness, substance abuse, poverty, and violence. These workers research and analyze policies, programs, and regulations. They identify social problems and suggest legislative and other solutions. They may help raise funds or write grants to support these programs. (Bureau of Labor Statistics, 2000)

The Career Timeline

As psychological and social beings, we are influenced by events and experiences in the past, the present, and even by expectations regarding the future. We have numerous associations and conceptions about various jobs, occupations, and careers. Our views and expectations about possible career paths are affected by our family-based attitudes and early school experiences. For example, suppose that as a fifth grader you had difficulty learning how to convert fractions to percentages. Your classmates seemed to catch on rather quickly. At that time, you concluded that you "cannot do math." Thereafter, you approached math problems with reluctance, uncertainty, and anxiety. You avoided mathematics courses and, whenever possible, let others solve math problems for you. You remained interested in science, however, until the eighth grade when you realized that some forms of science (e.g., chemistry and biology) required mathematics. At that point, you concluded that you "cannot do science" either. Later, when a guidance counselor suggested that test results indicated your aptitude for, interest in, and suitability for the profession of medicine, you were shocked. In fact, you had long dreamed of becoming a medical doctor. However, rather than incorporating this new information and reconsidering your conclusions, you decided that you could not possibly achieve your goal because of all the math and science that would be required as a premed major and subsequently in medical school.

Unfortunately, this is a common story, especially among girls, women, and members of certain racial and ethnic groups. People often reach conclusions about themselves, their talents and abilities, and their potentials fairly early in life. When the conclusions are favorable and optimistic, the effects can be quite beneficial indeed. When they are unfavorable and pessimistic, they may impede a person's growth and development in pervasive and perfidious ways. Such an individual might be reluctant to engage in learning activities due to self-limiting expectations and fear of failure. Fortunately, people can transcend limiting conclusions about their abilities, talents, and potentials—if they are aware of them and willing to invest the time and effort required.

Conducting self-assessments and gaining self-awareness may be approached from several perspectives. We addressed some of these in Chapters 2 and 3. In addition, you may prepare a career timeline[7] to organize important events or experiences related to your personal and professional development. Typically, learning accomplishments, achievements, and awards are recorded in chronological order over the course of a designated period of time. So are negative experiences that may have left you feeling fearful, ashamed, embarrassed, hurt, or angry.

Creating your own career timeline may enhance self-understanding, especially if you actively reflect upon its relevance for your present and potential learning activities. The basic elements of a career timeline include: (a) a long, solid line to reflect a period of time (e.g., your life), (b) perpendicular, intersecting, or angled lines that indicate the dates of selected events, and (c) brief descriptions of those relevant events or experiences linked to the dates. You may enhance these basic elements in numerous ways. For example, you may use a plus sign (+) to characterize events that enhanced your growth. You could use a minus (–) sign to identify events that diminished your personal and professional growth.

As a social work student, you might prepare such a timeline—preferably at the beginning of your academic program—and then make appropriate adjustments during your formal studies and afterward throughout your professional career. An example of a career timeline is shown in Box 4.2. For illustrative purposes, we refer to the student as Maria Sanchez,[8] an imaginary B.S.W. student.

Notice how the career timeline helps Maria organize significant events and experiences in her personal and professional development. She could elaborate on several aspects of the timeline in narrative fashion.

Preparing a Professional Résumé

As you begin to clarify a general career direction within the broad field of social work—one that matches your values and interests, personality characteristics, personal and lifestyle preferences, and career self-concept—we encourage you to prepare a professional résumé. You might start

---

[7] Adapted from Chapter 2 of *The Social Work Skills Workbook*, Third Edition, by Barry Cournoyer. Copyright © 2000 Brooks/Cole—Wadsworth.

[8] Maria Sanchez is a fictitious person as are some, but not all, of the agencies, organizations, and schools referenced in both the illustrative career timeline and résumé. The city of Indianapolis, Ben Davis High School, and the Indiana University School of Social Work are real entities.

by reviewing and reflecting upon your talents and abilities, areas of special knowledge, skill or expertise, and experiences you have had that might help prepare you for your chosen career.

Identify the subject areas you have mastered through formal or informal education, training, hands-on experience, or independent learning. Consider the courses, workshops, and seminars you have completed that relate to your chosen career direction. Try to identify the skills and abilities you possess that may, in some way, apply to a career in social work. Also note your achievements and accomplishments, as well as your work and volunteer experiences. Reflect upon the favorable effects or the outcomes of your efforts and activities. This information as well as the career timeline that you prepared earlier should help as you begin to develop a professional social work résumé.

There are several possible résumé formats. Each form emphasizes certain dimensions of experience. A *chronological résumé* highlights employment, volunteer, and educational experiences over time. To prepare a chronological résumé, identify your position titles and describe your roles, duties, and accomplishments. Specify the names and locations of organizations where you worked, volunteered, or matriculated. Place more recent experiences before earlier ones (i.e., reverse chronology).

Chronological résumés easily reflect progression within a field of study or an area of work and service. When identified organizations are well known and highly regarded, and when previous positions are relevant to the position sought, such résumés can be quite impressive. They are less useful when there are noticeable gaps or inconsistencies in your history, when frequent changes are apparent, when you are making a career change, and when you prefer to downplay your age. Chronological résumés are widely used. They are relatively easy to prepare and they are familiar to search committees, human resource personnel, and prospective employers. This form may be most appropriate when you want to continue to work in a certain field of service and can show successive accomplishments within the field.

Chronological résumés do have disadvantages. Gaps in employment and unrelated job experiences are readily apparent, and specialized knowledge, skills, and abilities are difficult to highlight. Nonetheless, because of its common usage, the chronological résumé deserves serious consideration.

Functional résumés represent a marked departure from the well-known chronological résumé. They emphasize strengths and achievements within the context of general professional goals. They are probably most useful for people who seek a career change or for those who have engaged in relatively unrelated employment, volunteer, and educational activities. To prepare a functional résumé, organize your experience in terms of functional skills, qualifications, and related accomplishments. Knowledge, skills, and abilities that you have gained through all forms of employed, academic, and volunteer experience are highlighted more than job titles, positions, employers, dates, and locations. Functional résumés are perhaps most advantageous for people who have limited work experience, have noticeable gaps in employment, or are seeking a position in a different field or area. Through the functional résumé, you present a case that your knowledge, skills, and abilities can be transferred to your desired position. In effect, you coherently organize your talents within the context of career directions and objectives that resembles the needs and goals of prospective employers.

Of course, there are disadvantages as well. If you have not carefully identified a career path or have yet to reflect upon and identify your knowledge, skills, and abilities, you may find it difficult to prepare an effective functional résumé. Also, savvy employers may be cautious about

BOX 4.2	MARIA SANCHEZ, B.S.W. STUDENT CAREER TIMELINE

1975 (March)	I was born on March 25, 1975. My mother had 8 years of formal education. My mother's father reached the 6th grade when he went to work to support his family. My family was Spanish speaking with some fluency in the English language. My parents, grandparents, and other relatives had high hopes for me.
1980	I began kindergarten with excitement and anticipation.
1980–1981	Unfortunately, my excellent Spanish speaking skills were devalued by my non-Spanish speaking kindergarten teacher. I soon became fearful of school where I was expected to talk exclusively in English.
1981–1985	I became a quiet, reclusive, and withdrawn student.
1986	Some children called me "stupid," "dumb," and "retarded." I began to wonder if they were right.
1987	A new teacher joined the faculty. She referred me to a school social worker. The social worker was wonderful. She provided support and understanding. She even spoke in Spanish! She arranged for me to take a whole battery of psychological, aptitude, and intelligence tests (Spanish versions). The test results indicated that I had well-above average verbal and math aptitudes, and a high IQ. The psychological tests also revealed that I was experiencing a great deal of school-related stress and depression.
1987–1988	My social worker informed the principal and the teachers of my abilities and potential. She arranged for special tutoring in English speaking and writing, and she met with me three or four times each week to help me address my fears and increase my self-confidence. Within a few months, I felt much better about myself and began to enjoy school.
1988–1992	My grades dramatically improved. I became an honor student and the teachers often showed their affection and appreciation for the high quality of my work.
1993 (June)	I became valedictorian of my class and delivered the graduation address in excellent English punctuated by references in Spanish. I was accepted by several fine colleges and won one large and two small scholarships.
1993–1994	I began college and performed exceptionally well in my first year. I earned high honors.
1994	During the summer, my mother became seriously ill. I decided to drop out of college to work full-time and provide personal care to my mother.
1994–1998	I worked for 4 years in child welfare services. I learned a great deal about policy and services for children, especially those from low-income families. I became familiar with various state, local, federal, and private programs that provide aid to children and their families. In addition, I developed considerable expertise in the use of computer applications relevant for social services organizations. I learned how to word process and design and use both spreadsheet and database programs. Largely due to my expertise with such computer applications, I was promoted to the position of Social Service Assistant to the Director of the Agency.
1998 (Spring)	When my mother died, I decided to return to college to pursue a degree in social work. I applied to the B.S.W. program at Indiana University and was accepted.
1998 (August)	I took my first social work course and learned about the social work portfolio. All students must submit a final version of their portfolios to the B.S.W. program director during the final semester of their senior year.
1998–1999	I completed my sophomore year with high honors and joined the social work student association.

1999–2000	During my junior year, I took several more social work courses; and completed my first B.S.W. field practicum in an agency that serves homeless persons affected by persistent mental illness and substance misuse.
1999–2000	I felt extremely comfortable as a social work student. I liked my colleagues and my professors. I ran for and was elected president of the Social Work Student Association.
2000–2001	During my senior year, I enrolled in advanced social work classes. I performed extraordinarily well.
2000–2001	I served in a child welfare agency for my senior field practicum.
2000–2001	I continued to love my work with children and their families. Before graduation, I was offered a part-time job at my practicum agency and was then asked to apply for a full-time social worker position following graduation.
2001–	I continue to serve as a child and family services social worker at the agency where I completed my senior year practicum. I enjoy the work enormously. The agency highly values my bilingual skills and has promoted me twice since graduation. At this point, I am beginning to consider applying for admission to a graduate social work program, perhaps one that offers a doctoral degree.

applicants who submit such résumés because of their familiarity with the more widely used chronological résumé.

A third form of résumé, the *targeted résumé,* is most applicable for people seeking specific positions within a relatively narrow field of work, study, or service. Ideally, you would prepare a unique targeted résumé for each and every position you seek. This form of résumé is sometimes referred to as a *combined résumé* because it incorporates elements of the functional and the chronological résumé in a manner that focuses on your capacities and potentials for success in a specific position. Targeted résumés are most useful when you know exactly what you want, when you do not mind preparing a slightly different version to accompany each application, and when you can show how your talents and experiences match the needs of your prospective employer. There are numerous advantages to targeted résumés. They include all the commonly expected information in a form that highlights knowledge, skills, and abilities that pertain to a particular position.

Some disadvantages exist as well. As you might expect, preparation of a targeted résumé requires a great deal of careful planning and a lot of work. You must know your career directions and understand your talents and abilities. Care must be taken to avoid redundancy. And some revision and editing are usually required for each and every distinct position sought. Of course, access to modern word-processing computer equipment and high-quality printers makes preparation and revision of targeted résumés easier that ever before.

A Résumé for Your Social Work Portfolio

A résumé is an important component of a social work portfolio. We have combined portions of all three formats (chronological, functional, and targeted) to provide you with maximum flexibility throughout your professional career. At different points, you may simply extract various sections and edit them to prepare different versions for different purposes. Try to keep the length of your résumé to four or five pages. A 10-point font and one-inch margins are standard. You may single space the résumé but use space separators to distinguish sections and use bold to highlight headings. We recommend the format in Box 4.3 for your social work portfolio.

Box 4.4 presents an example of a résumé that a social work student might prepare for use in the months preceding graduation.

Exercises

Independent Learning Exercises

4.1   Review the six personality orientations (RIASEC) as outlined by Holland. Log onto the World Wide Web and go to www.ncsu.edu/careerkey/ to complete the online version of Career Key, an instrument developed by Dr. Lawrence K. Jones based on Holland's RIASEC model. Your score will be calculated for you free of charge. Alternatively, you may complete the Holland Self-Directed Search (SDS) and receive the results online for a small charge at www.self-directed-search.com. Or you may complete the Holland Occupation Themes instrument online at www.doi.gov/octc/holland2.html—the Web site of the United States Department of the Interior.

Once you have completed one or more of these instruments, determine your three-letter Holland occupation code by identifying the three most highly rated dimensions in descending order (e.g., *RIS*). You may go to the Indiana Career and Postsecondary Advancement Center (ICPAC) Web site at icpac.indiana.edu/directsearch.html and insert your three-letter Holland code to retrieve a list of occupations and professions that match your profile. Alternately, you may review the *Dictionary of Holland Occupational Codes*[9] at your library or career center. This dictionary has a complete listing of occupations cross-referenced by Holland codes.

Word process a short essay concerning the implications of the results for a career as a social worker. As you consider the results of these instruments, however, be sure to keep in mind that information from additional sources would help support or challenge the findings. Also remember that the range of positions and roles within the profession of social work is so vast that people reflecting various personality orientations can usually find a niche that fits them well.

4.2   Turn to the Social Work Interests Instrument (SWII) presented in Appendix 5. Follow the instructions to gain a general sense of your level of interest in various social work jobs or roles. If there is a form or kind of social worker that is not identified, add it to the instrument. After you have completed the SWII, reflect upon the results.

4.3   Use the guidelines and descriptions presented in this chapter to word process a career timeline. We recommend use of the "create a table" feature of your software program.

4.4   Build on your career timeline by word processing a brief essay that describes your preferred social work career path—the general directions and themes within social work that you would like to pursue over the course of your professional life. Follow that with a succinct one-paragraph, word-processed description of your ideal social work position—the

---

[9]The *Dictionary of Holland Occupational Codes* (DHOC) (3rd ed.), (1996) by Gary D. Gottfredson and John L. Holland (Lutz, FL: Psychological Assessment Resources, Inc.) is the most recent edition.

job you would most like to have following completion of your academic studies. In another paragraph, discuss the knowledge, skills, and abilities that you think you would need to fulfill the duties and responsibilities of the ideal position. Finally, prepare another paragraph or so in which you discuss your own current suitability and readiness for the ideal position you would like to seek. Discuss the knowledge, skills, and abilities that you now have that match the needs of the ideal social work job. Identify those you will need to develop or strengthen and discuss the challenges and obstacles that you might face in securing your ideal position. Discuss how you might overcome them.

4.5   Use the recommended format to word process a draft of a résumé for inclusion in your social work portfolio.

4.6   Following completion of your first draft of the résumé, assess its quality through reference to the following guidelines:

- Overall Appearance: Does it appeal to you? Do you want to read it? Is it easy to read? What impression does it create?
- Contact Information: Are your name, address, phone numbers, and e-mail address clearly presented on the front page? Do your name and a sequential page number appear on each page of a multipage résumé?
- Content: Does the content clearly describe your qualifications, skills and abilities, accomplishments, and experiences? Is the content organized thematically or chronologically according to the chosen résumé style? Is the writing style crisp? Are words and phrases written efficiently?
- Relevance: Has extraneous information been eliminated? Are salient job-related accomplishments, skills, and experiences prominently noted?
- Length: Is it long enough to include everything you want known, yet short enough to be read easily and completely?

4.7   Reflect upon your résumé and ask yourself how you might improve it—not only in terms of its format and presentation but, more important, in regard to the kinds of learning and experience as well as the knowledge and skills that you might develop during the course of your academic studies that could contribute to your qualifications for your social work career and ideal position.

Collaborative Group Learning Exercises

4.8   Discuss among your group your conception of an ideal social work position. Explore with your colleagues the knowledge, values, and skills you will need to develop to be prepared for service in your ideal position. Discuss the courses, training, workshops, or other learning experiences that could help you become better prepared. Consider how you might use the assignments within your social work courses to maximize learning in the areas you wish to develop.

4.9   Share the draft of your résumé with at least one other group member. Imagine you are employers reviewing applicants' résumés. From that perspective, rigorously but constructively critique one another's materials. Make written notes about your colleague's feedback.

Personal Information

- Name
- Addresses (Current and Permanent)
- Telephone Numbers
- E-mail Address
- Web Site Address

Professional Aspiration

- Identification of Desired Professional Position
- Expected Roles and Responsibilities

Education (in reverse chronological order)

- School/Institutions/Programs Attended
- Locations (City, State/Province, Country)
- Dates of Attendance and Dates of Graduation or Completion
- Degrees, Certificates, Diplomas Earned
    - List your highest degree first. Titles of your dissertation, thesis, or senior project may be included.
- Major, Minor, Areas of Concentration or Specialization
- GPA, Class Rank, or Status (Optional)
- Knowledge, Skills, and Abilities Acquired

Professional Experience (in reverse chronological order)

- Agency, Organization, Group, Company (where employed)
- Job or Position Title
- Roles and Responsibilities
- Knowledge, Skills, and Abilities Acquired
    - Omit summer or short-term jobs unless relevant.

Career-Related Experience (in reverse chronological order)

- Agency, Organization, Group, Company (where volunteer or practicum/internship experience occurred)
- Status or Role
- Duties and Responsibilities
- Knowledge, Skills, and Abilities Acquired

Publications and Presentations

- Publications
    - Include completed works or those in press. Be sure to identify those that relate specifically to the duties and responsibilities of the desired position. You may also include pertinent unpublished papers (e.g., a major paper for a social work course). Cite your written works in the form customary to your field. In social work, the American Psychological Association's style is commonly used (1994). Organize your written works in chronological order (i.e., older before more recent works).
- Presentations
    - If you have made many presentations, you may wish to select those that are most relevant for your desired position.

Extracurricular Interests and Activities

- Professional Associations
    - You may include committee assignments, professional memberships, consulting activities, and leadership positions.

- Community Service Activities
  - Include community service activities that enhance or support professional experience. If you have engaged in many such pertinent activities, you may separate them into subsections.
- Awards and Honors
- Hobbies, Avocations, Interests

References

Although you may choose to insert a simple statement that "references will be furnished on request," we recommend that you include the name, degrees, title, organization, address, and phone numbers of specific persons. Typically, you would include the names of three to five people. Include people who know you and your work well, who are up to date on your activities and responsibilities, and who will speak/write very positively about you. Be sure to seek and secure their consent before you use them as references.

Supplemental Information (optional)

In this optional section, you may include any additional pertinent information that does not naturally fit in earlier sections. However, we recommend that you avoid references to marital status, children, health, physical appearance, age, date of high school graduation, and salary requirements.

Signature, Date

Portfolio Exercises

4.10 You now have a draft version of your résumé to add to your developing social work portfolio. You also have an increasingly clear sense about a career path and an ideal social work position. Indeed, you have already word processed several paragraphs about these subjects. At this point, it would be useful to copy and paste several of those word-processed passages to create a practice version of a cover letter that might accompany a résumé if you were to apply for your ideal social work position. After you have integrated previously word-processed content, edit the letter to improve its quality.

A cover letter is a business letter directed to a potential employer that expresses your interest in employment with their organization. (Please refer to Appendix 6 for a sample cover letter.) The cover letter accompanies your résumé, serving to introduce you and describe your suitability for a particular position (Kaplan, 1994).

Use the same font, or typestyle, to word process both your résumé and the cover letter. The coordinated appearance yields a polished, professional-looking submission. Often, you may be able to use the same résumé for different applications; however, each cover letter should directly relate to the specific job you seek. If there is an advertisement or job description, refer to it in your letter and indicate how you meet the requirements. This enables employers to more easily include, rather than exclude, you for further consideration. A well-prepared cover letter helps ensure that your résumé is read.

Begin the cover letter with one or two sentences that reflect your desire to apply for the position. Follow these with a paragraph that promotes your qualifications and abilities and discusses the goodness-of-fit between you and the requirements and responsibilities

BOX
4.4   RÉSUMÉ

Maria Sanchez, B.S.W. Student

192107 Alimingo Ave., Apt 12B
Indianapolis, Indiana, USA 46260

317-274-0001 (Home)
317-274-6705 (Office)
Email: *msanchez@emailnet.com*

Professional Aspiration

Social Work in Public or Private Child and Family Services Agency
I seek employment as a social worker in a child and family services agency. I wish to provide direct social work services to low-income and poverty level children and families. I have a special interest in service to racial and ethnic minorities, single-parent families, and children and families affected by abuse, violence, and substance misuse. I desire a position where I may provide individual, family, and group counseling as well as case management and advocacy services.

Education

B.S.W. (Expected May 2001), Indiana University School of Social Work, Indianapolis, Indiana, 3.70 G.P.A.

Certificate in Case Management (Expected May 2001), Indiana University School of Social Work, Indianapolis, Indiana
During my B.S.W. and case management studies, I developed knowledge and skills for interviewing children, adolescents, and family members. I learned to provide strengths-based case management, information and referral, and advocacy services to low-income children and adolescents. I developed individual, family, and group counseling skills. I learned to assess quality and effectiveness of social work services and to identify and use best practice approaches in my professional practice.

I learned to understand and appreciate the significance of diversity among individuals and developed individual and group counseling skills for service to persons affected by substance misuse and addictions. Special note: I am extremely fluent in both English and Spanish.

Diploma (June 1993), Ben Davis High School, Indianapolis, Indiana, 3.55 G.P.A., Valedictorian
During my high school studies, I discovered for the first time that I possessed talents and abilities as a student. I learned that I could think logically and analytically at a sophisticated level. I also found that I could speak articulately and persuasively with other people in both small and large group contexts. Perhaps most important, I learned to write well in English. I wrote more than a dozen articles for the school newspaper; numerous essays, and several larger papers for my courses. My teachers submitted two of my essays in statewide competitions. I placed third in the first competition and won first place in the other.

I was selected valedictorian of my senior class and delivered a speech at graduation ceremonies. I was also awarded one large and two small college scholarships based on my high school academic performance.

Professional Experience

Social Service Assistant (Part-Time), Child and Family Services Center, Indianapolis, Indiana, October 2000–Present
At this point, I have served as a part-time social service assistant to the director of the Child and Family Services Center for approximately 4 months. This appointment resulted from my field practicum experience. My field instructor has been impressed with my performance as a social work student intern. She learned of my previous work experience and my skills in computer database construction. She recommended me to the director who subsequently employed me on a part-time basis. In this role, I am assisting the agency director in the development and improvement of administrative and management services. In particular, I am helping to design and implement a computerized management and information system (MIS).

Child Welfare Specialist, Family Outreach, Indianapolis, Indiana, June 1994–August 1998
As a child welfare specialist with Family Outreach, I provided information, education, and referral services, along with case coordination services to at-risk children and the families. The children were at-risk of or had previously experienced forms of physical or sexual abuse and neglect. I negotiated and coordinated the activities of multiple service providers for each child and family. I also initiated group services for both at-risk children and their family members. For instance, I developed a reading-for-fun group program that resulted in a significant grade improvement (at least one letter grade) for all participating at-risk children.

During my last 2 years with the agency, I assumed some supervisory responsibilities for other child welfare specialists. I developed a computerized database to organize and coordinate several aspects of the child welfare specialist activities. Among others dimensions, the database enabled the input of demographic data, service goals, intervention contacts, contacts with collateral source and progress toward goal achievement for all clients. In addition, I included a capacity to organize and coordinate the work schedules of the full- and part-time child welfare specialist staff. During my term as supervisor, the rate of staff absences decreased by about 30% and turnover decreased by more than 25%.

Career-Related Experience

Social Work Student Intern, Child and Family Services Center, Indianapolis, Indiana, August 2000–Present
I am currently completing a two-semester field practicum experience with Child and Family Services Center, Indianapolis, Indiana. In my role as student intern, I provide services to children and families experiencing a wide range of social issues, including substance misuse, domestic violence, juvenile delinquency, truancy and academic problems, sexual offenses, along with mental-health-related concerns such as eating disorders and self-destructive and self-mutilating behaviors. Because of my previous child welfare experience, I have been encouraged to assume considerable responsibility for information, education, referral, and counseling services. I serve as a member of the case management team for approximately ten client families. I help to coordinate services and, with about five families, provide direct services as well. I received an evaluation of "excellent" for the first semester and expect to do so for the second semester as well.

Social Work Student Intern, Midtown Homeless Services, Indianapolis, Indiana, August–December 1999
During the fall semester 1999, I completed a field practicum experience with Midtown Homeless Services. Through that experience, I learned about the nature and extent of homelessness in the Indianapolis area. As part of the practicum, I accompanied a social worker and nurse on mobile visits to persons living in city alleyways, under bridges, and in automobiles. I helped to identify needs and link homeless individuals and families with shelters, food pantries and kitchens, health and mental health, substance misuse, and social services. I also participated in the preparation and presentation of testimony to city and state officials and members of the state legislature. In addition, I helped to write sections of a grant proposal to help fund services to the homeless population. I received an evaluation of "excellent" from my field instructor, and I received a special letter of recognition and recommendation from the agency director for my efforts during the field practicum.

Volunteer, Hispanic-American Center, Indianapolis, Indiana, May 1992–Present
While in high school, I volunteered to tutor Spanish-speaking children and adults in the English language. Over the years, this project has grown so that I teach a group of approximately 15 people two evenings each week. I have received much recognition for this service and continue to find it extraordinarily satisfying.

Publications and Presentations

Sanchez, Maria. (unpublished). Low-income, female-headed families in the inner city. Paper submitted in partial fulfillment of the requirements for the SW410 Human Behavior and the Social Environment course. Indiana University School of Social Work, Indianapolis, Indiana, Spring 1999.

Sanchez, Maria. (unpublished). A review and analysis of contemporary child and family welfare policies: Implications for low-income children and families. Paper submitted in partial fulfillment of the requirements for the SW430 Social Policy and Services course. Indiana University School of Social Work, Indianapolis, Indiana, Fall 1999.

Sanchez, Maria. (2000). Developing a computerized management information system for child welfare services. Paper presented at the annual conference of the Indiana Chapter of the National Association of Social Workers, Indianapolis, Indiana.

Sanchez, Maria. (under review). Evidence-based best practice approaches for service to children and families affected by domestic violence. *Child Welfare: The Journal of the Child Welfare League of America.*

(continued)

BOX
4.4   **RÉSUMÉ (*CONTINUED*)**

Extracurricular Interests, Activities, and Awards

Outstanding Social Work Student Award, Indiana University School of Social Work, May 2000

National Association of Social Workers, Student Member, 1999–Present

Social Work Student Association, Indiana University School of Social Work, President, 1999–Present; Member 1998–Present

Hispano-American Student Association, Indiana University Purdue University Indianapolis (IUPUI), Vice-President, 2000–2001; Member 1998–Present

Valedictorian, Ben Davis High School, 1993

Hispanic-American Center, Indianapolis, Indiana, Volunteer Tutor & English Language Instructor, May 1992–Present

Student Editor, High School Newspaper, 1992–1993

References

Dr. Joseph Fisher, D.S.W.
Indiana University School of Social Work
902 West New York Street
Indianapolis, Indiana 46202\-5156

Adrian Romley, Director
Child and Family Services Center
1230 Wayward Way
Indianapolis, IN 46250

Dr. Warren Jamison
Family Outreach
431 N. Daniels Street
Indianapolis, IN 46202

_____   _____
Maria Sanchez, B.S.W. (Expected May 2001)   Date

---

of the job. Refer to your enclosed résumé. Conclude the letter with a short paragraph that expresses your appreciation for the opportunity to submit your résumé and apply for the position.

When the time comes to prepare an actual cover letter, address each letter to a specific person. Include his or her name and title. You might decide to send a letter and résumé to an organization that has not advertised or announced a position vacancy. If you do so, identify the person who should receive your materials. You might telephone the organization and ask to whom your application materials should be directed. Make sure to spell correctly the person's name and title as well as the name of the organization. Use Ms. rather than Miss or Mrs. unless you know for certain the preference of an addressee.

If you are unable to determine the person's gender, omit the courtesy title (e.g., Mr. or Ms.) entirely and simply use both the first and last name.

4.11 After you have created and edited your practice cover letter, review it carefully by considering the following questions. Use your responses to these questions to further revise and edit your cover letter.

- Is the purpose of your letter clearly presented?
- Are your qualifications, credentials, and accomplishments summarized and is their match with the requirements of the position highlighted?
- Are your special or unique qualities, talents, and abilities described in such a way that an employer could readily see how you could help meet organizational needs and goals?
- Are the outcomes or results (e.g., a personal interview, or an opportunity to meet and discuss the position further) of the cover letter and accompanying résumé clearly stated?

The presentation of the cover letter is just as important as the content itself. Check for spelling, grammatical, and punctuation errors. Word-processor spell-check programs are far from foolproof. For example, suppose you type "manger" when you mean to use "manager." The spell-check program will not catch it because "manger" is correctly spelled.

Preparing Personal Learning Plans

In Chapter 3, you considered the fundamental social work knowledge, values, and expertise required of all social workers. Using materials related to your learning experiences, you undertook a fairly comprehensive assessment of your current proficiency in the social work knowledge base. You began to collect documents to support aspects of your learning, and you gained an awareness of your own general learning needs. In Chapter 4, you began to consider your professional career directions and identified an ideal social work position. You prepared a résumé and practiced writing a cover letter that might accompany a job application. Through these activities, we sincerely hope you developed a greater appreciation of the significance of lifelong learning, which we had explored in Chapters 1 and 2, as well as a better understanding of the value of the social work portfolio. Although we requested that you begin to collect several materials related to your learning style, needs, and goals, we have not yet asked you to develop specific learning plans. We want you to do so in this chapter (see Box 5.1).

Personal Learning Plans

A personal learning plan (PLP) is a written document that contains descriptions of one or more learning goals, a rationale for their selection, specific learning objectives, action plans (e.g., activities and experiences) by which to pursue the identified learning goals and objectives, and means and processes for evaluating progress. Most social workers are extremely familiar with the processes of planning or contracting in their service to clients (Cournoyer, 2000, pp. 265–310). The format of a personal learning plan is similar to social service plans and contracts. They differ in that the purpose and content address the development of your own knowledge, values, and expertise rather than those of your clients.

You may know teachers who write extensive "lesson plans" and some professors who create course syllabi that describe in detail what they expect their students to learn. However, you probably do not routinely create lesson plans or syllabi for your own learning goals and objectives.

Personal learning plans represent a way to do for yourself what your best teachers have done for you. The process enables you to identify what you want to learn, why you want to learn it, how you plan to learn it, and how you intend to show you have learned it. Personal learning plans may be termed learning contracts, learning agreements, personal development plans, personal audits, professional learning plans, personal action plans, or learner profiles. Regardless of the term used to describe them, personal learning plans require that you, the learner, assume personal responsibility for identifying learning needs and goals and developing plans to pursue them. Rather than a teacher, professor, supervisor, or boss, you are at the center of the learning process. You become the active, self-directed learner that we discussed early in Chapter 1. Thus, you may alter and revise your personal learning plans as your wants, needs, and circumstances change.

BOX

5.1   CHAPTER PURPOSES

The purposes of this chapter are to introduce you to the components of a personal learning plan and to help you learn to develop plans by which to pursue, assess, and document progress toward your specific learning goals and objectives.

Goals

Following completion of this chapter, you should be able to:

- Discuss the essential elements of a high-quality personal learning plan
- Understand the significance and relevance of various learning opportunities
- Prepare a personal learning plan
- Evaluate the quality of a personal learning plan

There are many reasons to create personal learning plans. As you know, we believe that continuing lifelong learning is an essential requirement for competent, ethical, and effective social work service. Personal learning plans contribute to your growth and development as a professional by helping you direct and organize your energy for learning in a purposeful way. Although many social workers may be intrinsically motivated to learn to better serve their clients, we recognize that extrinsic factors also influence behavior. Social work students may be required to develop or complete a personal learning plan upon admission to their program or in one or more of their classroom or practicum courses. Practicing social work professionals may prepare and implement learning plans to meet changing job requirements, demonstrate accountability, respond to political imperatives, or pursue new career interests and aspirations.

The idea of personal learning plans or learning contracts is not entirely new. For example, all incoming students who enroll in the higher education program of the North East London Polytechnic develop individualized learning contracts that outline the necessary steps and experiences required for the diploma (Challis, 2000). Although they are advised by and consult with faculty, students in the program assume a great deal of personal responsibility for determining their own learning goals, undertaking learning experiences, and demonstrating achievement.

Learners who prepare and implement personal learning plans tend to *learn how to learn*. They tend to become active, self-directed, motivated learners able to continue learning on their own long after they earn their degrees. As the locus of responsibility for learning shifts from the teacher toward themselves, students experience a greater sense of control, empowerment, and personal satisfaction (Huff & Johnson, 1998). They also acquire skills for lifelong learning. Students determine what to learn and why and how to learn it. In effect, they become their own teachers.

Although more research is certainly needed, there are indications that favorable outcomes occur when students prepare and use personal learning plans (Bullock, 1999; Phillips, Prue, Hasazi, & Morgan, 2000). They are used quite extensively in the education of medical doctors, especially in Great Britain (Challis, 2000) where portfolio-based learning is popular (Challis, 1999). However, personal learning plans and other forms of self-directed learning are not universally accepted among college faculties (Wilcox, 1996). Despite growing awareness of the principles of adult learning (Knowles, Holton, & Swanson, 1998), the developing body of evidence related to the nature of effective teaching and learning (Chickering & Gamson, 1987), and the need for lifelong learning skills in the third wave information age (Barr & Tagg, 1995; Toffler, 1983; Toffler & Toffler, 1995), some professors are reluctant to adopt innovative teaching and assessment methods.

Our conception of a personal learning plan includes the following major sections: *learning goals, rationale* (for learning), *learning objectives, action plans, social support,* and *evaluation.* These six dimensions represent a format or outline through which to organize and prepare learning plans. However, the components are also processes that may be repeated in relation to different learning needs over a lifetime. We reflect them when we determine our own learning goals; clarify reasons and purposes for their selection; convert our general goals into specific objectives; plan activities to pursue, support, and evaluate progress toward achieving those objectives; implement the plan; assess outcomes; and as an outgrowth, identify new learning needs and goals as we begin the processes all over again. You may notice the similarity of the PLP component processes to the Shewhart cycle (Plan-Do-Study-Act) and the learning wheel (Reflect-Connect-Decide-Do) mentioned in Chapter 2.

Learning Goal(s)

A learning goal is a general description of the knowledge, value, or expertise that the learner wishes to develop or aspires to attain. Typically, the learning goal is a sentence or two in length. The learner addresses the general question, "What do I wish to learn?" Hence, the formulation of a learning goal involves a process of personal reflection. As Malcolm Knowles suggested, you "diagnose your learning needs" (Knowles, 1998, p. 212) and convert them into goals. The goals often relate to career aspirations. Most social work students, for example, want to graduate from an accredited program and university. They want to pass the social work licensing examinations necessary to become licensed to practice their profession. Some aspire to a particular form of service, such as school social work, and establish goals in that arena.

Goals are defined in broad terms and may refer to any form of learning. All areas and dimensions of knowledge and information may be included. Attitudes, values, beliefs, and emotions of any sort might be a focus for learning. And of course, so might skills and abilities of every kind. The range of possible learning goals is virtually infinite and is limited only by the boundaries of your imagination.

Rationale

The rationale includes the fundamental or primary reasons that motivate the learner to pursue the learning goal. Usually a paragraph or two in length, the rationale provides impetus and energy to the endeavor. The learner addresses the general question, "Why do I wish to learn this?"

The learner's rationale often emerges as a natural part of the reflection or "learning diagnosis" process that results in the identification of a need or gap in learning that, in turn, leads to a learning goal. As Malcolm Knowles suggested, "A learning need is the gap between where you are now and where you want to be in regard to a particular set of competencies" (Knowles, 1998, p. 212).

You may already be aware of certain learning needs. A performance evaluation, the results of knowledge, aptitude or vocational testing, or perhaps your own personal reflections may have led you to identify several gaps between where you are now and where you would like to be.

Learning Objectives

Each learning objective represents a specific, precise, and detailed description of exactly what you plan to learn. They are derived from your learning goals. Learning objectives are written so that progress toward their achievement is relatively easy to assess, measure, or evaluate. Typically, an action verb (e.g., describe, do, classify, perform, list, analyze, conduct, create, write, demonstrate, prepare, compare, define, predict) is used and a time frame specified to provide clarity and precision. You may choose an action verb that matches one of Bloom's taxonomic levels (i.e., recollection, comprehension, application, analysis, synthesis, or evaluation).[1] The learner addresses the question, "In clear, specific, precise, and descriptive terms, what exactly do I want to learn to accomplish a part of my general learning goal?" A learning objective might be phrased in the following manner: "Within 1 month of today's date, I will be able to write a high-quality service plan for each of my agency clients."

Learning objectives are not efforts you intend to make or things you plan to do. Rather, they are aspects of knowledge, values, attitudes, or expertise that you seek to learn. Ideally, the written description includes an action verb to facilitate assessment of accomplishment. Identify no more than a few learning objectives for each learning goal. More than three or four become cumbersome.

Action Plans for Learning

An action plan includes learning activities, experiences, tasks, or steps that, if completed, lead to the achievement of learning goals and objectives. If you were a teacher, these would be your "lesson plans." In planning activities and experiences, the learner asks, "How can I accomplish my learning goals and objectives? What do I do? What resources do I need?" In effect, the learner selects from among the array of sources, means, and methods of learning the approaches that reflect the greatest probability of success.

The learner designs activities and experiences most likely to be effective and efficient. Therefore, you incorporate information about yourself (e.g., psychological type, personality profile, learning style preferences, nature and degree of self-motivation, circumstances) to increase the probability that you will attempt and complete the activities and, in turn, achieve your objectives as efficiently as possible.

Regardless of the nature of the learning activities and experiences you select, we urge you to include the creation or preparation of some form of evidence of learning—preferably a learning product. Documented evidence of learning may occur in many forms. We mentioned several in Chapter 3: academic transcripts; certificates, licenses, diplomas; course syllabi; workshop and seminar brochures; and performance evaluations, test results, or other forms of feedback. We also described some products that you might prepare or complete as part of a learning experience. Examinations, essays, research papers, theses, posters, slide shows, and audio- or videotapes of oral presentations are examples of learning products commonly completed during academic coursework. Such products are also important in self-directed learning. They constitute concrete

---

[1] See Appendix 7 for an array of action verbs organized in accordance with Bloom's taxonomy.

evidence of learning. We recommend that you create at least one learning product that may be assessed or evaluated for each major learning goal you pursue.[2]

Social Support

Social support involves the guidance, encouragement, external motivation, and emotional understanding of other persons or groups. You will probably need the support of others to complete your personal learning plans, especially if your goals are challenging and your activities difficult. In identifying social supports, you address questions such as: Who can and will provide social support and guidance during this learning process? Who might advise me? Who would be emotionally supportive and encouraging? Who could motivate me if I were to lose interest and energy?

Participants in a study group may provide social support. Indeed, colleagues in your collaborative learning group are likely candidates. Perhaps a tutor, mentor, adviser, or supervisor could do so as well. An increasing number of agencies and institutions are attempting to become "learning organizations" (Senge, 1990, 1992; Senge et al., 1994). Such organizations provide incentives, encouragement, and various other forms of support for individual and group learning. Ideally, people who agree to provide social support are knowledgeable about you and your circumstances, respect your desired learning goals, and appreciate your individual characteristics and learning style. Personal qualities associated with social support include well-developed listening skills, the ability to communicate empathically, an optimistic attitude, and a capacity to provide constructive feedback and advice in a nonjudgmental and noncontrolling manner.

Evaluation

Evaluation refers to the tools, instruments, or processes learners use to assess or measure progress toward achievement of learning goals and objectives. In preparing a personal learning plan, the learner anticipates the nature of the learning products that will result and considers the criteria that could be used to assess quality and outcomes.

In planning for evaluation, address question such as: How will I determine that I have learned what I wanted to learn? What evidence will I use? What assessment criteria or guidelines will I use to evaluate the quality of my learning (e.g., judge the products I prepared)? If the learning objectives have been precisely written, assessment processes tend to fall logically into place.

Typically, the evaluation process relates to three pieces of tangible evidence that can be included or referenced in a social work portfolio: (a) one or more learning products that naturally result from learning activities, (b) evaluation of the quality of the learning products, and (c) a reflective assessment of the learning process.

Two forms of learning product evaluation would be ideal. First, a self-assessment demonstrates an ability to evaluate the quality of your own work from a reasonably objective perspective. Be sure to demonstrate a willingness to think critically and analytically about the learning product. Second, evaluations undertaken by one or more colleagues or mentors add an independent dimension to the process. In the evaluations, include reference to established criteria or

---

[2] Please note that we encourage a learning product for each major learning goal. It would be inefficient to prepare learning products for each and every learning objective. We assume that a learning product that reflects evidence of progress toward or achievement of a learning goal simultaneously supports accomplishment of the learning objectives associated with the goal.

standards of quality. You could create or adopt an assessment rubric to guide the review of your products. For example, you might adapt a general rubric (see Box 5.2) to assess various learning products.

Finally, and perhaps most important, learners reflect upon the entire process and outcomes of their learning experience. Perhaps in the form of a short essay or a personal diary entry, learners consider what they learned—both planned and unplanned. Sometimes the most important learning is serendipitous, occurring more or less as a by-product or side effect of efforts to learn something else.

In reflecting on the process, learners consider how they learned what they did. They identify learning activities that seemed most natural and effective. They imagine what they might do differently if they were to begin the learning process all over again. They ponder how their learning connects or relates to their personal lives, professional careers, and long-term aspirations. A form of critical thinking, such reflection is fundamental to all learning, especially lifelong learning. Indeed, as you reflect upon learning experiences of all kinds, you might consider the principles for learning in social work proposed in Chapter 1. They may serve to guide the self-reflective process as you consider, for example, how you demonstrated humility, empathy, and fairness; courage; honesty and integrity; clarity, accuracy, and precision; relevance; intellectual sophistication; and logic during the course of your learning activities.

Although we view these components as essential to a personal learning plan, you may add others to better suit your individual needs and preferences. Before you begin your own plan, however, we would like to offer a few simple guidelines:

- Identify learning goals that are personally and professionally meaningful to you. As much as possible, try to choose goals that have more intrinsic than extrinsic value. If you are required to learn something new because of external factors, try to frame or conceptualize the learning goals so they become personally relevant.
- Try to discover personal reasons for pursuing learning goals. Identify why and how such learning can benefit you and contribute to your own growth and development. If possible, link new learning to previous experience and connect it to long-term personal or professional aspirations.
- Assess your personal motivation and capacity to implement the personal learning plan. If your motivation or capacity is low, figure out why. Perhaps the goals are not personally or professionally meaningful enough for you to invest the time and energy. Or you may be so pressed with responsibilities that even highly relevant learning goals cannot motivate you to proceed at this particular time. Attempt to address and resolve the potential motivational obstacles before you begin. Otherwise, you will probably find the experience unsatisfying and unsuccessful.
- Make the plan simple and easy to follow. Outlines usually work better than extensive narratives.
- Describe objectives clearly, precisely, and specifically so you can easily determine if you are making progress. Use action verbs and include a time frame. Adopt learning objectives that are challenging enough that you have to work hard to achieve them. Learning something that is too simple or easy will probably leave you feeling unsatisfied. However, be careful not to make the objectives so difficult that you cannot realistically accomplish them. That usually leads to frustration and sometimes to defeat.

BOX
5.2
GENERAL ASSESSMENT RUBRIC FOR LEARNING PRODUCTS

	Amateur	Novice Professional	Intermediate Professional	Advanced Professional
Focus and Relevance	The product reflects little attention to learning objectives or is irrelevant to identified goals and purposes.	The product reflects some attention to learning objectives and is relevant to identified goals and purposes.	The product reflects considerable attention to learning objectives and is clearly relevant to identified goals and purposes.	The product consistently reflects careful attention to learning objectives and is definitely relevant to identified goals and purposes.
Accomplishment	The product fails to represent or reflect evidence of achievement of learning objectives and accomplishment of goals and purposes.	The product represents or reflects evidence of achievement of some learning objectives and partial accomplishment of goals and purposes.	The product represents or reflects convincing evidence of achievement of all learning objectives and satisfactory accomplishment of goals and purposes.	The product represents or reflects outstanding evidence of achievement of all learning objectives and exceptional accomplishment of goals and purposes.
Depth and Elaboration	The product consistently reflects insufficient depth of learning and a general failure to elaborate upon significant aspects.	The product reflects depth of learning in some but not all significant areas and ability to elaborate upon some but not all significant aspects.	The product reflects considerable depth of learning in most significant areas and ability to elaborate upon most significant aspects.	The product reflects exceptional depth of learning in all significant areas and ability to elaborate upon all significant aspects.
Critical Thought or Analysis	The product reflects little evidence of critical thought or analysis.	The product reflects some evidence of critical thought or analysis.	The product reflects considerable evidence of good quality critical thought or analysis.	The product consistently reflects substantial evidence of advanced levels of critical thought or analysis.
Organization and Presentation	The product lacks coherent organization and is presented in a poor or unprofessional manner.	The product reflects some organizational structure and is generally presented in a professional manner.	The product reflects a clear and coherent organizational structure and is consistently presented in a professional manner.	The product reflects an extremely clear and coherent organizational structure and is presented in an exceptionally professional manner.

- If at all possible, phrase your learning objectives in positive or affirmative terms. Describe what you plan to learn rather than what you hope to unlearn or discontinue.
- Design your action plans so that you can carry them out independently. Build in plenty of social support, but try to avoid situations where your learning is dependent on the competence or actions of others. If at all possible, rely primarily on yourself.
- Describe your action plans in the form of specific steps or experiences. Incorporate the activities with a schedule or routine so that they become natural and automatic.
- Personally and publicly commit to take action. Tell one or more people in your social support network about your goals and plans.
- As you undertake your action plans for learning, regularly ask yourself how well they are working. Reflect upon the impact of your activities. If they are not going well, revise your plans by creating smaller or simpler steps, adapting the learning activities to better suit your circumstances, or by changing or increasing your social support.
- Create a tangible product as a result of your learning activities. Such evidence can serve multiple purposes, especially if you also engage in an assessment of the product.
- Assess the product or outcome, assess the process, and reflect upon the experience as

The Process

If you take a few minutes to reflect upon your life, your dreams and aspirations, and yourself as a person and social being, you could easily identify a great many things you would like to learn. For most of us, it would be a very long list indeed! Significant people in your life might also contribute. For example, in response to the question, "What would you like me to learn?" a social work colleague might suggest, "I'd like you to learn more about group counseling skills and techniques so you can join me as co-leader of my Tuesday night group." A supervisor might request that you "learn to manage your time better and submit your paperwork when it's due." An administrative might ask you to "learn how to do short-term counseling to serve more people in a cost-effective manner." A client might indicate, directly or indirectly, that she would like you to "learn more about my culture and its traditions." Or clients who struggle with a certain issue (e.g., alcohol abuse) might subtly reveal that they wish you knew more about "how to help me stop drinking."

A friend might say something such as, "I'd like you to learn to speak Spanish so we can take a trip to South America." Or "I wish you would learn to be on time. I hate it when you keep me waiting." A spouse might request that "you learn to be more affectionate with me." Or "I wish you would learn to relax and enjoy life. You're too serious." A teenage son or daughter might say, "I wish you'd learn to really listen to my side of things before you start yelling at me."

Many factors motivate people to learn. Certainly, application to a university program of study usually reflects a desire to learn, or at least to achieve. Because they involve the potential for success as well as failure, classroom or field practicum courses also tend to increase motivation. Most of us would rather pass than fail. The licensing examinations motivate most social work graduates to learn—at least enough to pass the test and secure a license to practice social work. In most locales, licensed social workers are legally required to engage in a certain amount of professional learning and earn a number of continuing education units (CEUs) each year. Many professionals participate in conferences, workshops, and seminars that enhance their knowledge and expertise and often pique their interest to learn even more.

Other conditions may inspire us to learn as well. For example, you might feel obligated to further your learning following a professional error or mishap that adversely affected a client's well-being. Conversely, you might try something new and do so well that you become excited to learn even more. Interactions with other people and life experiences of all kinds may lead to heightened interest in learning. Some social workers maintain a diary or journal to keep track of events and thoughts about their professional service. They often record ideas about how they might continue to grow, learn, and develop. Learning journals enable social workers to refer back to earlier experiences, organize ideas into major learning themes, or develop priority lists that can lead to learning goals and action plans.

Perhaps because social work affects the lives and well-being of real human beings, students and practitioners can usually easily identify large numbers of professionally relevant learning goals. Suppose, for example, you are interested in school social work. You might consider learning goals such as these:

- "I'd like to learn how to assess the risk of violence among schoolchildren."
- "I want to learn how to plan and lead an anger-management group experience for schoolchildren."
- "I hope to learn how to recognize indicators of alcohol and drug misuse among schoolchildren."
- "I need to learn how to report information about possible child abuse or neglect to state authorities."

Consider this last learning goal. Most people are well aware of the legal obligation to report indications that a child might be at risk of abuse or neglect. However, the specific reporting requirements may vary from one locale to another. A social work student interested in this topic might prepare a personal learning plan as in Box 5.3.

Personal learning plans exemplify self-directed, lifelong learning processes that extend throughout your professional career. Consistent with the principles of andragogy and lifelong learning, they may be used to pursue all kinds of learning. Whether your goals relate to knowledge development, values clarification, attitudinal change, or the development of skills and abilities, learning activities guided by personal learning plans tend to be personally meaningful, relevant, stimulating, and productive. Furthermore, they result in documentary evidence of your learning—in the form of products, assessments, and reflections. Personal learning plans and the products that result from their implementation represent important materials for inclusion within a social work portfolio.

Exercises

In this chapter, we introduce and discuss the processes associated with developing plans for learning. The following exercises should help you prepare a personal learning plan of your own.

Independent Learning Exercises

5.1 Earlier in this chapter, we suggested that most social work students could easily identify several pertinent professional learning goals. We now ask you to do precisely that. Please take a few minutes for reflection and then identify one learning goal that would be especially relevant and useful as you pursue your career aspirations. Word process that goal in general terms.

5.2 Learning goals may be classified within various categories: knowledge (developing awareness, understanding, or comprehension), values and attitudes (clarifying or strengthening principles that guide actions; adopting preferred beliefs, perspectives, or views), or skills (developing or refining internal abilities such as analysis, synthesis, or evaluation and external abilities such as application of theoretically or empirically based knowledge in social work practice). Determine which categories best reflect your learning goal. Then, to gain some practice experience, write or word process one learning goal for each of the other categories. Ensure that each goal is personally or professional relevant.

5.3 Now review the learning goals you have generated. Choose one that you consider the most important or timely in terms of your own personal or professional learning needs. Incorporate it within the learning goal section of your personal learning plan. Following that, word process a one- to two-paragraph rationale for its selection. When complete, incorporate it within the rationale section of your developing personal learning plan.

5.4 Now use your rationale as a context from which to develop specific learning objectives that relate to your chosen learning goal. Word process one to four learning objectives. Use an action verb and ensure that each objective refers to a learning outcome. Include a time frame for the accomplishment of your learning objectives.

5.5 At this point, you have established a few clear and precise learning objectives. Brainstorm about possible activities, experiences, actions, or steps that you could take to accomplish them. Keep your personal characteristics, priorities, circumstances, and preferred learning styles in mind as you develop your action plans for learning. Try to identify learning activities that match these factors to increase the probability that you take action to accomplish the learning objectives.

Once you have generated a substantial array of potential learning activities, review and edit to make it manageable. Word process the revised list and include it within the action plan section of your personal learning plan.

5.6 Reflect upon the action plans you proposed and the learning objectives you selected. Consider the individuals and groups that might serve as helpful sources of social support as you undertake the learning activities. Identify each person by name or role. Briefly describe how they might individually or collectively be helpful. Write or word process your response and include it within the social support section of your personal learning plan.

5.7 Consider how you might evaluate progress toward the accomplishment of your objectives. Identify learning products that you could prepare that would represent clear evidence of learning. Ponder evaluative criteria that you could adopt that might guide your assessment of the quality of the learning products. Select what you consider to be the preferred learning products and the most relevant evaluative criteria. Write or word process a two- or three-paragraph summary of your plans for evaluation and incorporate it within the evaluation section of your personal learning plan.

5.8 You have now completed a draft version of a personal learning plan. Review the plan. Determine if it flows logically and coherently from beginning to end. Edit or revise as necessary. When complete, place it within a folder for later inclusion within your social work portfolio.

SAMPLE PERSONAL LEARNING PLAN

1. Learning Goal

I want to learn how to report information about possible child abuse or neglect to proper authorities.

2. Rationale

I want to become school social worker. I am presently enrolled in a field practicum experience in a grammar school. The school serves children in kindergarten through the third-grade age range. It is a wonderful placement and I am learning a great deal. The school social worker and the school principal, of course, know how to report indications of child abuse and neglect. They have done so dozens of times over the past few years. However, they do not have a written policy or procedure to guide school personnel in submitting such reports. I am interested in learning about the laws and legal requirements. I want to learn exactly which authorities are legally authorized to receive the reports. I would like to learn about the proper format for filing reports of possible child abuse or neglect. I want to know about the legal and ethical responsibilities of school social workers. I would like to learn what experts in the field advise about best practices. I want to know what the research literature suggests about various approaches to the identification and report of indications of child abuse and neglect.

I am interested in this topic for several reasons. I am motivated because I know child abuse and neglect are major social problems affecting thousands of children each year. I want to help prevent the abuse and neglect of children, but I also want to do so in the right way—legally as well as morally and ethically. I also want to learn how to file necessary reports without damaging my professional relationships with the affected children or their families.

3. Learning Objectives

Within 1 month of today's date, I will be able to:

a. Describe and accurately discuss the state laws and regulations regarding child abuse and neglect, including the duty to report information pertaining to possible abuse or neglect of children.
b. Describe and accurately discuss the state laws and regulations regarding any special duties social workers, teachers, and school administrators might have when in possession of information regarding the possible abuse or neglect of a child.
c. Identify the specific state or local authorities to whom a report of possible child abuse or neglect should be submitted and the preferred form in which it should be filed.
d. Discuss and analyze the professional practice guidelines and ethical principles that school social workers should consider in submitting a report regarding possible child abuse or neglect.
e. Prepare a draft of a Policy and Procedures Manual for Reporting Information Pertaining to the Possible Abuse or Neglect of a Child.

4. Action Plans for Learning

I plan to review the state laws (legal code) and make copies of all passages that pertain to child abuse and neglect, including the reporting requirements. I will also review and make copies of all passages that relate to the profession and practice of social work, particularly those sections, if any, that refer to special duties of social workers in circumstances that involve the possible abuse or neglect of children. I plan to examine and duplicate those sections of the state code that pertain to the offices or departments of state and, if applicable, local governments responsible for the protection of children. Once I identify the appropriate governmental officials, I plan to arrange meetings with them to learn about their processes and protocols. I will ask to review written materials used by those officials to guide their actions when reports are received. I will also request copies of preferred or required forms for reporting possible child abuse or neglect.

In addition, I plan to research the professional literature, consult with social work experts in the field, and confer with professionals at national centers or institutes concerning best practices and ethical principles that might help identify, assess, and report indications of possible child abuse or neglect. I intend to discuss with school social workers, teachers, and principals what might ideally go into a school child abuse and neglect reporting manual. I will correspond with pertinent organizations to request relevant information. I plan to locate manuals, documents, or related materials from other schools, state departments of education, professional associations, advocacy organizations, and the federal government. The documents may serve as useful references as I prepare a manual for our school.

5. Social Support

I intend to share my plans with my supervising school social worker, other social work students placed in school settings, and members of my study group. I will also ask my favorite social work professor, who knows a great deal about school social work and child and family welfare services, to serve as adviser for the project.

6. Evaluation

The major documentary evidence of achievement of my learning goal and objectives will be the school manual that I prepare. It will constitute a major learning product. The criteria that will guide my assessment of the quality of the policy and procedures manual are as follows:

a. How well is the manual organized, written, and edited?

b. How accurately and completely does the manual present the information needed by social workers, counselors, teachers, and school administrators to report indications of possible child abuse or neglect in a legal and professional manner?

c. How well do the suggested reporting processes reflect respect for the civil rights and human dignity of the affected persons while protecting the safety of potentially vulnerable children?

d. How well researched, documented, and referenced is the manual?

In addition, I will ask social workers, teachers, school counselors, school administrators, and the principal to provide feedback concerning the draft version of the manual. I plan to review and consider their comments in order to revise and improve its quality. I intend to complete a final version of the manual at least 2 weeks prior to the conclusion of my field practicum.

Finally, approximately 1 month following submission of the final version of the manual to school officials, I will write a one- to three-page reflective essay about the learning experience.

Collaborative Group Learning Exercises

5.9   As a group, discuss your experience of constructing a personal learning plan. What did you find useful? What seemed to be of little value? What do you think about the format for organizing the plan? How might you change it to make it more pertinent and relevant to you?

5.10 Share your personal learning plan with other members of your group. Compare your learning goals, rationales, learning objectives, action plans, social supports, and plans for evaluation. Discuss commonalities and distinctions. Provide constructive and supportive feedback. Write a few notes concerning themes and issues that emerge during the conversation. Also note how you might improve your own personal learning plan.

5.11 Discuss your views about the implications of personal learning plans for lifelong learning as a social worker. Explore with one another the factors and circumstances that might help you and your colleagues use personal learning plans during the remainder of your university studies and subsequently as practicing professionals.

Portfolio Exercises

You have completed a personal learning plan that you may include as part of your expanding collection of materials for your social work portfolio. Before moving on to the next chapter, however, we ask you to consider a few issues.

5.12 Consider the ideal social work position that you identified in Chapter 4. Generate a list of learning goals that would help you be highly prepared to assume the roles and undertake the activities that would probably be required in your ideal position. Word process those goals to ensure that they remain a focus for learning.

5.13 Reflect upon the implications of the learning goals that relate to your ideal social work positions for the classroom or field practicum courses that you are now or soon will be taking. Generate the outline of a plan by which you might adapt the requirements of the courses to help you pursue the learning goals associated with your ideal position. For example, suppose you must prepare a major paper for a social work practice course. Consider how you might use that assignment to meet your own learning goals, perhaps by writing a paper on a topic that relates directly to your ideal social work position. Word process an outline of your plan.

COMPILING AND ASSESSING YOUR SOCIAL WORK PORTFOLIO

You have reached the last chapter of this book. You are nearly finished! Through your efforts, you have collected and prepared many of the materials needed to complete your social work portfolio. You have also made a great deal of progress toward becoming an energetic, self-directed, and collaborative lifelong learner.

During earlier chapters, you thought about the implications of the knowledge explosion and the learning revolution for social workers of the 21st century. You reviewed several principles for lifelong learning and considered guidelines for collaborative group learning in social work. You explored your multiple intelligences and considered your emotional intelligence as well. You interpreted your psychological type and identified your preferred learning styles. You considered the fundamental knowledge, values, and skills needed by contemporary social workers and assessed your proficiency in key dimensions of the general social work knowledge base. You also began to collect pertinent documents that serve as evidence of learning and assessed some of your own learning products. You considered your personality characteristics in relation to your occupational choice and began to explore a general career path within the profession of social work. You identified an "ideal social work position" and considered some of the roles and functions you might assume in that position. You created a career timeline and then prepared a draft of a résumé and evaluated its quality. You also prepared a practice cover letter that might accompany your résumé in a job application. You developed and evaluated a personal learning plan and then considered some of the learning goals that might match the roles and functions of your ideal social work position. You have accomplished a great deal indeed!

As you move toward the conclusion of this book, we ask you to prepare a few more pieces and then integrate the elements into a working version of your social work portfolio. Following that, we would like you to undertake a comprehensive assessment of the entire dossier. Based on your assessment, you may improve, refine, and polish the social work portfolio to serve one or more important professional purposes (see Box 6.1).

Compiling the Components of Your Social Work Portfolio

In the introduction to this book, we discussed some of the purposes for social work portfolios and identified components that might be included. The process of compilation begins by reconsidering your major purposes for this version of the portfolio. Different purposes lead to different forms. If you are primarily preparing the portfolio to complete the requirements for a classroom course, a field practicum experience, or an academic program of study (e.g., B.S.W., M.S.W., Ph.D.), then you compile a social work portfolio to meet these academic expectations. If you recently graduated and are preparing a portfolio to help organize your initial career planning and job search, you tailor the components to match these purposes. An experienced practitioner using

---

BOX

6.1   **CHAPTER PURPOSES**

The purposes of this chapter are to help you compile, assess, and improve the quality of your social work portfolio.

Goals

Following completion of this chapter, you should be able to:

- Prepare or edit materials for inclusion in your portfolio
- Incorporate relevant materials in the portfolio
- Assess, revise, and improve the quality of your social work portfolio
- Plan for future use and further development of the portfolio

---

the portfolio to maintain an organized and documented approach to continuing professional education and career development adopts another form.

Throughout the compilation process, keep the primary purposes clearly in mind. Despite the variations that naturally occur, we propose the following generic portfolio format. Although geared to the exercises contained within this book, the format can be easily adapted to serve the needs and purposes of most social work students and practitioners (see Box 6.2).

Title Page

The social work portfolio contains a well-designed title page. Even if you prepare your portfolio in electronic form (e.g., Web site or slide-show presentation), you will probably need a printed version as well. Typically, the materials are organized within an accordion-style expandable folder that contains tabbed sections. An oversized three-ring binder can be used, although some documents (e.g., copies of diplomas or transcripts) may be difficult to read because of the punched holes. If you do use a binder, find one that allows you to insert a title page on the outside cover. The outside title (i.e., cover) page typically includes a title (e.g., *Maria Sanchez: A Social Work Portfolio*), your name as the author of the portfolio, and place and date of publication. If the portfolio fulfills a requirement for an academic course, field practicum, or degree, you also include the name of the college or university and school or department. If the title page serves as the outside cover, another copy is placed within the portfolio as well. The inside title page follows the submission letter. A title page might appear as shown in Box 6.3.

The Submission Letter

Your submission letter precedes the inside title page because it is not officially part of the portfolio. Address the letter to the pertinent person or office (e.g., prospective employer or academic official). The dated submission letter is usually one page in length. In the letter, you inform the recipient that the accompanying portfolio contains selected materials and request that it be reviewed. The submission letter might appear as shown in Box 6.4.

BOX 6.2   **THE SOCIAL WORK PORTFOLIO: GENERIC FORMAT**

    I. Title (Cover) Page
   II. Submission Letter
  III. Inside Title Page
  IV. Table of Contents
   V. Introduction
  VI. Résumé
 VII. Personal Statement
VIII. Learning Products and Self-Reflective Assessments
  IX. Summary
   X. Appendixes
      A. Diplomas, Certificates, Licenses
      B. Transcripts (or Transcript Summary)
      C. Course Syllabi
      D. Performance Appraisals and Evaluations
      E. Letters of Reference and Recommendation
      F. Personal Learning Plans
      G. Career Timeline
      H. Additional Materials
         a. Responses to Exercises
         b. Short Essays
         c. Learning Journal Entries

Table of Contents

A table of contents follows the title page and summarizes the sequence in which the materials are presented within the portfolio. Include the page number where each major section begins. This enables reviewers to turn quickly to pertinent materials. The table of contents might appear as shown in Box 6.5.

Introduction

The introduction to your social work portfolio follows the table of contents. Introduce the recipients or reviewers to the contents by summarizing the purposes for your preparation and submission of the portfolio. Address the "why" question: Why have you invested all this time and energy in preparing the portfolio? Also discuss "how" you have organized the portfolio. Describe the structure or format into which you have compiled your materials.

Discuss the focus and rationale for the portfolio. If you prepared it to complete a course or degree requirement, indicate as much. However, you might also add personal and professional reasons. For example, you might discuss how you are using the portfolio for career planning purposes or as part of your search for a social work position.

Following a discussion of the purposes and rationale, you may describe the contents of the portfolio and the sequence in which you present them. In essence, you elaborate on the submission letter with a few sentences related to each of the portfolio sections. You might mention the

SAMPLE TITLE PAGE

MARIA SANCHEZ:
A SOCIAL WORK PORTFOLIO
Submitted to

INDIANA UNIVERSITY
SCHOOL OF SOCIAL WORK
Indianapolis, Indiana

by

Maria Sanchez, B.S.W. Student

In partial fulfillment of the requirements for the
Bachelor of Social Work degree

April 1, 2001

SAMPLE SUBMISSION LETTER

Maria Sanchez, B.S.W. Student
192107 Alimingo Ave., Apt. 12B
Indianapolis, Indiana, 46260
Tel. (317) 274-0001

April 1, 2001

Director, B.S.W. Program
Indiana University School of Social Work
902 West New York Street, Suite ES4138
Indianapolis, Indiana 46202-5156

Dear Director:

Enclosed please find my social work portfolio. I submit it in partial fulfillment of the requirements for the Bachelor of Social Work degree. The portfolio contains the following:

1. Table of Contents
2. Introduction
3. Résumé
4. Personal Statement
5. Three Major Learning Products with Corresponding Assessments
6. Summary
7. Appendixes containing copies of my high school diploma and related certificates, a current B.S.W. transcript, selected course syllabi, evaluations from B.S.W. Field Instructors, and three letters of reference

I believe I have met or exceeded all of the requirements for the social work portfolio as described in the B.S.W. Student Handbook. I understand that the assessment committee will review my portfolio and provide written feedback within 30 days.

Should you have any questions, please feel free to contact me at 317-274-0001.

Sincerely,

Maria Sanchez
B.S.W. Student

---

titles of the learning products you have included and, because they are so vital, write a few words about each of them. The introductory section is usually no more than two pages in length. A sample introduction is presented in Box 6.6.

Résumé

The résumé follows the Introduction. In Chapter 4, we described the nature, uses, and format of a professional résumé. We will not repeat that information other than to reemphasize the importance of a high-quality résumé for the social work portfolio.[1] Along with your selected learning products, the résumé best reflects your potential as a professional social worker.

---

[1] For an example, refer to Maria Sanchez's résumé in Chapter 4.

Personal Statement

The personal statement follows the résumé and precedes the learning products. The statement, usually 5–10 pages in length, enables you to describe and elaborate on your personal history, professional development, qualities, and philosophical approach to social work and service. The nature of the personal statement varies according to the purposes of the version of the portfolio. Indeed, there are some circumstances where a social worker might omit the personal statement from the portfolio. If you are preparing a portfolio for a classroom or field course or for an academic program, a personal statement is usually advised or required. Especially toward the conclusion of a social work program (e.g., B.S.W., M.S.W., Ph.D.), most students have a well-developed perspective about the profession and the service it involves. As a result of the exercises in this book, you probably also have a sense of who you are as a person, as a learner, and as an emerging professional. The personal statement provides an opportunity to present yourself within this context.

Although the topics explored within the personal statement may vary, we encourage you to build on work done for earlier exercises in this book. In particular, we suggest that you elaborate on the following facets of your personal and professional life.

Autobiographical Sketch   In this section, you might describe significant aspects of your personal background. Your career timeline and résumé should serve as useful reference material for preparing the autobiographical sketch. For example, you might describe how you became interested in the pursuit of higher education in general and social work in particular. You could identify significant people or events that led you to follow your academic paths. You might describe how your personal motives, personality characteristics, and values relate to the mission and purposes of the social work profession.

Self-Assessment   You could, in narrative fashion, discuss your strengths and weaknesses as a learner and social worker. For example, you might describe how this academic program fits into your career aspirations and ideal social work position. You could refer to the exercises you com-

SAMPLE INTRODUCTION

Maria Sanchez:
A Social Work Portfolio

Introduction

The social work portfolio fulfills a major requirement for the Bachelor of Social Work (B.S.W.) degree at the Indiana University School of Social Work. I believe this portfolio accurately reveals the extent of my growth during the B.S.W. program. It also documents my readiness for service as a professional social worker in the field of child and family services. I believe these materials reflect a depth of knowledge and expertise needed to provide competent case management, advocacy, and counseling services to low-income and poverty-level children and their families.

I have organized the portfolio into sections indicated by numbered colored tabs. The portfolio contains a current résumé, a personal statement of my philosophical approach to the profession and practice of social work, three papers I prepared during the B.S.W. program along with a self-assessment of each, and a summary. I also include appendixes that contain copies of my high school diploma and two certificates that pertain to other educational experiences, a copy of my current B.S.W. transcript, copies of selected course syllabi, a personal learning plan related to a major professional learning goal, and copies of the summary evaluations of my performance in two field practicum courses. Three letters of reference are also enclosed.

Recognizing the importance of the papers as evidence of learning, I include three. I wrote one for a sophomore year Social Policy course, another for a junior year Human Behavior and the Social Environment course, a third for a senior year Social Work Practice course. In the social policy paper, I address issues that pertain to contemporary child and family policies and practices. In the HBSE paper, I explore the topic of low-income, single-parent, female-headed families who live in inner city neighborhoods. In the advanced social work practice paper, I consider best practice approaches for service to children and families affected by domestic violence. I view this paper as my best work to date. Recently, I submitted a revised version to <u>Child Welfare: The Journal of the Child Welfare League of America</u>. I should learn whether it has been accepted for publication within the next month or so.

Accompanying each of these written products is a short assessment essay. In the essays, I reflect upon the strengths and weaknesses of each paper and discuss what I could do to improve its quality.

This portfolio contains a great deal of information concerning my readiness for a career in social work. Preparation of the portfolio required much time and effort. However, the process helped me clarify and solidify my goal to become a professional social worker specializing in services to low-income children and families affected by domestic violence and substance misuse.

---

pleted in Chapters 2, 3, and 4 to summarize aspects of yourself in terms of personal and personality characteristics, learning styles, and learning needs and goals. Importantly, you might discuss dimensions of the professional knowledge base where you are proficient and those that need further study. Some of the work you completed in Chapter 5 as you developed plans for additional learning may be useful here as well.

Personal and Philosophical Perspectives Following your autobiographical sketch and self-assessment, you might then discuss your personal and philosophical perspectives about the profession of social work and your approach to practice. You might, for example, discuss your views about the social work profession and the roles you envision for yourself. You could describe your personal philosophy about human behavior and the processes of change. You might discuss the practice approaches you value and describe the models you might use in helping the clients you would serve if you were to secure your ideal professional position. You might discuss your expectations about the future of contemporary society and describe how you plan to prepare for those anticipated changes.

This portion of the personal statement provides an opportunity to demonstrate your capacity to think critically and analytically at a conceptual level. Furthermore, it enables you to clarify for yourself, as well as for your readers, your philosophical approach to professional service.

Learning Products and Reflective Assessments

The products you prepare during the course of your formal and informal learning experiences are so valuable that they deserve a separate section within your portfolio. They represent the most tangible documentary evidence of your learning. Indeed, your social work academic program may require you to incorporate certain products in your portfolio. For example, your program may expect you to include a paper, report, essay, or examination you completed for courses from each major curriculum area. Students in your program may conduct senior projects that result in major integrative papers. You may be required to include the senior project paper within the portfolio. Some programs require a qualifying examination, essay, or paper for students entering the final stages of their studies. You may be expected to include your qualifying products in the portfolio. Different programs have different requirements to address their programmatic mission and goals.

If you are not required to include certain learning products as an academic course or program requirement, select a few examples of your best work. Choose products that best reflect evidence of your knowledge, values, and expertise for both general practice as well as for those functions and roles associated with your ideal social work position.

Each product, however, should be accompanied by a written reflective assessment. If you have not already done so, review your selected products and reflect upon their quality. Prepare a one- to two-page reflective assessment of each product. You might use a ready-made assessment rubric to guide your review (see Chapter 5 for a general version) or create your own. However, be sure to evaluate each of your products according to identifiable criteria or dimensions for assessment. Identify the strengths and weaknesses and discuss how you could improve each learning product.

Summary

The summary section provides an opportunity for you to reflect upon the entire portfolio and the processes associated with its preparation. You might describe the impact of the portfolio and some of the unanticipated outcomes. For example, the portfolio may have enabled you to recognize linkages among several curriculum areas and to integrate various learning experiences. Completion of the portfolio may have helped you organize documentary evidence of learning that may be used, with modest revision, to search for a social work position. The portfolio may have led to a realization that you have grown personally and professionally during the social work program. You could even report serendipitous outcomes of portfolio development, such as recognizing a special commitment to a certain social problem or a particular at-risk population group.

You might use the summary section to discuss goals and plans that have emerged as a result of the process. You could also describe how you intend to use your social work portfolio in the future (see Box 6.7).

<table>
<tr><td>BOX
6.7</td><td>**SAMPLE SUMMARY**</td></tr>
</table>

Maria Sanchez:
A Social Work Portfolio

Summary

The completion and submission of the social work portfolio represent a personal and professional hallmark. Although I prepared the portfolio primarily because it is required for the Bachelor of Social Work (B.S.W.) degree at the Indiana University School of Social Work, I gained a great deal through the process. Collection and assessment of learning products, review of transcripts and course syllabi, and examination of various performance appraisals and evaluations enabled me to reflect upon my strengths and weaknesses as a social worker. I was able to identify several additional learning needs and goals that I will pursue following graduation. For example, I realized that I do not have a sufficient understanding of childhood medical and psychiatric illnesses. While I possess a solid understanding of developmental processes and milestones, I need to learn much more about the biophysical and genetic factors that influence children and their families. I plan to enroll in a course offered through the School of Nursing to enhance my understanding in this area.

Overall, however, I believe the portfolio accurately reflects the quality and extent of my learning during the B.S.W. program. I am prepared to serve in the field of child and family services. I look forward to providing case management, advocacy, and counseling services to low-income and poverty-level children and their families. I also anticipate opportunities to further enhance my knowledge and skills through continuing professional education and supervision. I plan to take the examination for licensed social worker (L.S.W.) as soon as I meet all the eligibility criteria. Following that, I will explore the possibility of pursuing graduate education at the M.S.W. and perhaps the doctoral levels.

I am pleased with my social work portfolio. I believe it is organized and presented in a professional manner and accurately reflects the quality of my work during the B.S.W. program. If I had an opportunity to start over, I would begin the process of collecting and organizing portfolio materials at the beginning of my undergraduate studies. Indeed, I wish I had begun the process earlier in the B.S.W. program as well. I would have prepared a personal learning plan at the very beginning of the program. Had I done so, I might have selected a few different courses and I certainly would have approached all of them in a more focused way—incorporating my own learning goals as well as those identified in the syllabi. I also would have prepared a draft version of my personal statement at the beginning of my studies and then added to and revised it as a result of my learning experiences. Nevertheless, the social work portfolio enabled me to recognize my abilities as a adult learner and appreciate the importance for self-directed lifelong learning.

In the near future, I plan to adapt my portfolio to serve several purposes. In my search for employment in the field of child and family services, I will revise the portfolio to make it smaller and more directly related to my ideal professional position. For instance, I intend to remove two of the learning products and highlight the paper that addresses social work practice with children and families affected by domestic violence.

I hope to maintain a portfolio throughout my professional career. It will help me keep track of documents related to the continuing professional education requirements necessary to maintain a social work license. The portfolio will also be useful in a few years, when I apply to a social work graduate program.

Appendixes

The appendixes contain assorted materials to support or document information presented in the body of the portfolio. Various materials may be included within separate appendixes. For example, in one appendix, you could include copies of your diplomas or degrees, certificates, awards, and professional licenses. Another might contain copies of academic transcripts. A third appendix could be used to hold copies of various performance appraisals or evaluations. A fourth might contain one or more personal learning plans, and another might include various letters of reference or recommendation. A final appendix may be used for additional materials that do not logically fit within other sections.

Assessing the Social Work Portfolio

Various persons or groups may assess your social work portfolio. You may assess your own portfolio, or a colleague might do so on your behalf. Academic advisers and professors or perhaps members of a quality assessment committee could examine your portfolio. Prospective employers or members of admission committees (e.g., graduate programs or institutes) might do so as well.

We assess portfolios in much the same fashion as we do learning products. In general, three dimensions are considered: the purposes of the portfolio, the contents, and the form. Whether explicit or implicit, you hold certain purposes in mind as you prepare your portfolio. You also refer to these purposes to evaluate the overall quality of your portfolio. You ask yourself: How well does the portfolio fulfill its purposes? For example, suppose you prepare a portfolio to demonstrate your competence as a school social worker. If you incorporate within your portfolio clear and convincing evidence of your knowledge, abilities, personal suitability, and readiness for service as a school social worker, you have successfully fulfilled your purpose.

Other people who evaluate your portfolio may or may not consider your identified purposes in their assessment. We hope they do. However, they most certainly will consider their own. For example, if an admissions officer uses portfolios as part of the process of selecting graduate students for an academic program, that purpose will probably supersede your own. Ideally, your purposes and those of other portfolio reviewers are reasonably compatible. Indeed, you try to consider their purposes as you prepare different versions of your social work portfolio.

Portfolios may be assessed for formative or summative purposes. Formative assessment refers to the processes associated with improvement. For example, when academic advisers review students' portfolios and suggest areas for additional work, they are providing formative assessment. When a classmate reads the portfolio and recommends that you correct certain spelling and grammatical errors, she offers formative feedback. When members of a B.S.W. assessment committee review a random sample of anonymous student portfolios to identify areas of strength and weakness within the academic program and improve the quality of the curriculum, they engage in formative assessment. Alternatively, professors who assign a letter or numerical grade to a portfolio are adopting a summative approach to assessment. Similarly, employers engage in summative assessment when they review portfolios to make hiring decisions. When faculty in a school or department of social work evaluate students' portfolios and assign grades of pass or fail as a requirement for graduation, they do so in a summative fashion.

Purposes

The purposes of the social work portfolio as outlined in the introductory section are evaluated for clarity and relevance and are then used as dimensions for further assessment. Portfolios submitted to meet academic course or program requirements are reviewed in light of those learning goals and objectives as well. For example, suppose an accredited B.S.W. program designs and implements a curriculum intended to prepare its graduating students to demonstrate the professional abilities to:

1. Apply critical thinking skills within the context of professional social work practice.
2. Engage in ethical decision making within the values of the social work profession.
3. Practice without discrimination and with respect, knowledge, and skills related to clients' age, culture, class, disability, ethnicity, family structure, gender, national origin, race, religion, and sexual orientation.
4. Understand the forms and mechanisms of oppression and discrimination and apply strategies of advocacy and social change that advance social and economic justice.
5. Understand and interpret the history of the social work profession and its current structures and issues.
6. Apply the knowledge and skills of social work practice with systems of all sizes.
7. Use theoretical frameworks to understand individual development and behavior and the interactions among individuals and between individuals and families, groups, organizations, and communities.
8. Analyze, formulate, and influence social policies.
9. Evaluate research studies and apply findings to practice, and evaluate their own practice interventions.
10. Use communication skills differentially across client populations, colleagues, and communities.
11. Use supervision and consultation appropriate to social work practice.
12. Function within the structure of organizations and service delivery systems, and seek necessary organizational change. (Council on Social Work Education, 2001)

Portfolios might be used to assess an individual student's proficiency in these professional abilities. In the aggregate, student portfolios could also serve to indicate the degree to which the program achieves its curriculum goals and objectives. In reviewing student portfolios for either of these purposes, however, the identified abilities represent dimensions for assessment. Reviewers would consider, for instance, how well a portfolio demonstrates a student's ability to "apply critical thinking skills within the context of professional social work practice" (1) and "evaluate research studies and apply findings to practice, and evaluate their own practice interventions" (9). The remaining expected student learning outcomes would also be assessed during the review process. Various components within the portfolio (e.g., learning products and their assessments, field practicum evaluations, academic transcripts) would be used as indicators of proficiency in these abilities.

Contents

The contents of the portfolio are assessed for quality and relevance to the explicit or implicit purposes of the portfolio. The materials incorporated within the portfolio are identified and perhaps classified. The portfolio may be assessed holistically or dimensionally. A person adopting a holistic approach would consider the portfolio in its entirety and might provide general feedback or perhaps an overall rating or grade. A dimensional perspective involves assessment of various aspects of the portfolio. Specific feedback and perhaps a rating or grade may be assigned to each dimension of the portfolio. For example, a professor might identify "evidence of critical thinking and scholarship" as an essential aspect of portfolios submitted by social work students. By including learning products (e.g., research papers) and reflective assessments that incorporate analysis, synthesis, and evaluation, students address that dimension. Similarly, an employer might consider "depth and relevance of experience" as one factor to consider in examining a job applicant's portfolio. A portfolio containing a résumé that references pertinent professional experience along with copies of performance reviews and letters of recommendation from previous employers within the same field would likely be viewed with favor.

In considering the contents of a social work portfolio, reviewers address questions such as the following: What components are required or might reasonably be expected within a portfolio submitted for the identified purposes? Are those materials present? Are some important elements missing or incomplete? Are unimportant, extraneous, or irrelevant materials included—perhaps to fill up space? A simple "yes," "no," and "not applicable" checklist of components might be used, with space to add unexpected but relevant materials that were not required or anticipated.

Following an identification of the contents of the portfolio and a basic determination concerning their relevance, the quality of those components might be considered. For example, a professor could ask: What is the quality of the personal statement, the learning products, and their corresponding reflective assessments? Do they reflect the knowledge, values, and expertise needed by contemporary social workers? Do they exemplify qualities such as humility; empathy; fairness; courage; honesty and integrity; clarity, accuracy, and precision; relevance; intellectual sophistication; and logic? Do the contents of the portfolio demonstrate professionalism and, if so, at what level—novice, intermediate, advanced? Does the portfolio reflect growth and development over time? Is there evidence of increasing knowledge and ability?

The social work portfolio contains the documentation and supporting evidence needed to demonstrate your increasing readiness for professional service. Content assessment involves identification of materials, consideration of their relevance, and evaluation of their quality.

Form

The form of the portfolio (i.e., the quality of its preparation and presentation) is also considered part of the assessment process. Reviewers ask questions such as these: Is the portfolio logically and coherently organized, conscientiously composed, well written, and carefully edited? Has it been submitted in a timely fashion? Are there spelling or grammatical errors? Are names of persons and their titles accurately reported? Is the portfolio presented in an attractive, appealing, and professional manner? Is the table of contents accurate? Are dates, figures, and other facts correct and consistent (e.g., do dates reported in the résumé match those indicated on the academic transcript and diploma)?

Although an appealing presentation cannot make up for inadequate content, form indeed has an impact. And because the form of a portfolio is usually the initial impression, it may be lasting. An attractive, professional-looking portfolio often leads reviewers to look more carefully at the contents.

Portfolio Assessment Rubric

We introduced a learning product assessment rubric in Chapter 5. A similar rubric may be used to guide assessments of social work portfolios (see Box 6.8). However, even when the rubric accurately reflects the purposes for the portfolio, it is best used to stimulate reviewers' examination and evaluation of the materials. Rubrics seem to be most useful when they lead to a comprehensive, fair, and objective assessment, perhaps accompanied by a written narrative summary with comments and recommendations. They are least useful when they contribute to an unsubstantiated numerical rating or letter grade.

You may use the rubric to guide the review of your own social work portfolio or those of your colleagues. Other reviewers may adopt or adapt it to aid them in their consideration of portfolios as well. The dimensions identified in the rubric are general in nature. If you need a more specific version, incorporate additional factors to provide greater precision.

Whether you complete your own portfolio assessment or others do so for you, use the results to further your growth and development as a professional and to improve your portfolio. Reflect upon the assessment. Consider the validity, relevance, and utility of the feedback. Use the assessment information to reflect upon the nature and quality of the dossier. Following a period of reflection, develop plans to improve your social work portfolio to better meet your needs, goals, and aspirations.

Planning for the Future

Although the social work portfolio is submitted to various recipients (e.g., professors, assessment committees, admissions officers, prospective employers) in the form of a dossier, it actually remains quite incomplete. We envision the portfolio more as a process than a product—one that evolves and changes over time.

To address issues associated with anticipated stages of professional development[2] and help you achieve your career goals, we encourage you to update your social work portfolio regularly throughout your lifetime. Add pertinent materials (e.g., CEU certificates, performance appraisals, papers or reports you prepare) at least once each year and reconfigure the portfolio whenever you consider a significant change. For example, when you receive an award or promotion, assume a different position, seek a new job, or apply for admission to a graduate school or institute, remember to revise your portfolio accordingly.

As you anticipate maintaining and revising your social work portfolio, you may conclude that the time and energy required are not worth the effort. We believe that such a conclusion is both shortsighted and unwarranted. Regular updates typically require little more than inserting materials within existing folders. Even the process of reconfiguring the portfolio to address professional changes typically requires only a few hours, and perhaps even less if you have word processed and saved components (e.g., letter of submission, introduction, résumé, personal statement, learning products, reflective assessments, summary) that your prepared earlier.

Until you have personally experienced the benefits of having your own social work portfolio readily available for common professional purposes, you may underestimate its value. Once you realize how useful and timesaving it can be, you may find it difficult to overestimate its worth. Each year, when we must complete our annual self-reviews of academic performance, we recognize anew the utility of our own portfolios. We believe that you will find them just as helpful in your professional careers.

---

[2] Refer to Appendix 2 to review some stages of professional development.

BOX
6.8
ASSESSMENT RUBRIC FOR THE SOCIAL WORK PORTFOLIO

	Amateur	Novice Professional	Intermediate Professional	Advanced Professional
Purpose	Most major purposes of the portfolio are unidentified, irrelevant, or unclear.	Some major purposes of the portfolio are identified, relevant, and clear.	Most major purposes of the portfolio are identified, relevant, and clear.	All major purposes of the portfolio are identified, relevant, and clear.
Organization and Presentation	The portfolio lacks coherent organization and is presented in a poor or unprofessional manner.	The portfolio reflects some organizational structure and is generally presented in a professional manner.	The portfolio reflects a clear and coherent organizational structure and is consistently presented in a professional manner.	The portfolio reflects an extremely clear and coherent organizational structure and is presented in an exceptionally professional manner.
Relevance of Contents	The portfolio reflects little attention to the identified, required, or expected purposes. Some expected materials are missing or incomplete, and some irrelevant materials are included.	The portfolio reflects some attention to the identified, required, or expected purposes. Most expected materials are included, and most irrelevant materials are omitted.	The portfolio reflects considerable attention to the identified, required, or expected purposes. All expected relevant materials are included, and nearly all irrelevant materials are omitted.	The portfolio consistently reflects attention to the identified, required, or expected purposes. All expected and some additional relevant materials are included, and all irrelevant materials are omitted.
Quality of Contents and Evidence of Accomplishment	The portfolio fails to achieve its purpose. There is little evidence of progressive accomplishment or readiness for professional social work service.	The portfolio partially achieves its purpose. There is some evidence of progressive accomplishment and readiness for professional social work service.	The portfolio clearly achieves its purpose. There is substantial evidence of progressive accomplishment and satisfactory readiness for professional social work service.	The portfolio definitely achieves its purpose. There is convincing evidence of progressive accomplishment and superior readiness for professional social work service.

	Amateur	Novice Professional	Intermediate Professional	Advanced Professional
Professional Sophistication and Elaboration	The portfolio consistently reflects insufficient professional sophistication and a general failure to elaborate on significant aspects.	The portfolio reflects professional sophistication in some but not all significant areas and an ability to elaborate on some but not all significant aspects.	The portfolio reflects considerable professional sophistication in most significant areas and a clear ability to elaborate on most significant aspects.	The portfolio reflects exceptional professional sophistication in all significant areas and an outstanding ability to elaborate on all significant aspects.
Critical Thought or Analysis and Scholarship	The portfolio reflects little evidence of critical thought or analysis and scholarship.	The portfolio reflects some evidence of critical thought or analysis and scholarship.	The portfolio reflects considerable evidence of good quality critical thought or analysis and satisfactory scholarship.	The portfolio consistently reflects substantial evidence of advanced levels of critical thought or analysis and exceptional scholarship.
Honesty and Integrity	The portfolio reflects evidence of dishonesty or insufficient attention to matters of professional integrity.	The portfolio reflects no evidence of dishonesty. There are indications that matters of professional integrity receive some attention.	The portfolio reflects considerable evidence of honesty and satisfactory attention to matters of professional integrity.	The portfolio consistently reflects substantial evidence of exceptional honesty and conscientious attention to matters of professional integrity.
Self-Awareness and Self-Reflection	The portfolio lacks evidence of self-awareness or an ability to engage in self-reflection.	The portfolio reflects some evidence of self-awareness and emerging ability to engage in self-reflection.	The portfolio reflects considerable evidence of self-awareness and developing ability to engage in self-reflection.	The portfolio consistently reflects substantial evidence of high levels of self-awareness and exceptional ability to engage in self-reflection.

Conclusion

Congratulations! You have completed all but the final exercises of the last chapter of this book! We sincerely hope that as you progress in your professional career, you find the effort you invested helps you maintain a high-quality social work portfolio and continue your enthusiasm for lifelong learning. We trust you gained an appreciation for the complex professional demands that accompany the advancing information and technology age. We hope that you developed some clarity about your professional career aspirations and significantly increased your self-awareness. Indeed, we asked you to engage in numerous exercises related to the development of lifelong learning skills and abilities and the preparation of elements of your portfolio. We urged you to compile many materials and documents, assess them, and reflect upon their meaning and implications.

You have done a lot of work indeed! We believe it will benefit you for years to come. We also thank you on behalf of the clients you will serve and the profession of social work that you represent. We fully expect that you will be a more effective social worker as a result of your efforts.

Now, as you conclude this book, we ask you to complete a few final exercises. We hope they help you feel a sense of genuine satisfaction and encourage a commitment to maintain your social work portfolio as you continue to plan, assess, and document lifelong learning throughout your professional career.

Exercises

Independent Learning Exercises

6.1   Identify the major purposes for preparing a social work portfolio at this particular time. If you are doing so to fulfill a requirement for a course or academic program, be sure to consider the expectations that your professors have in mind. Word process one or two paragraphs that highlight those major purposes. You will use these passages for the submission letter, introduction, summary, and possibly some aspects of your personal statement for inclusion within your social work portfolio.

6.2   Identify the components that you want to or are required to include in your social work portfolio. Ensure that these components will meet the identified purposes.

6.3   Word process a title or cover page for your social work portfolio. Refer to Box 6.3 for guidance.

6.4   Word process a submission letter. Refer to Box 6.4 for an example. Copy, paste, and then edit passages you prepared in your response to Exercise 6.1. Follow that with a duplicate copy of the title page. (Note: This is the inside title page.)

6.5   Using the outline of components that you prepared for Exercise 6.2 as a starting point, type or word process a table of contents. Refer to Box 6.5 for an example. (Note: You may add page numbers later.)

6.6   Refer to the major purposes you identified for Exercise 6.1 to prepare an introduction to your social work portfolio. Refer to Box 6.6 for an example.

6.7   Review and, if needed, update or polish the résumé you prepared as part of your work for the exercises in Chapter 4.

6.8   Refer back to the pertinent sections of this and earlier chapters and then word process a personal statement that contains a biographical sketch, a self-assessment, and a discussion of your personal and philosophical perspectives. When complete, edit it carefully, ask for feedback from a colleague, revise if needed, and then include it within your portfolio.

6.9 Consider the purposes for the portfolio that you outlined in Exercise 6.1 and discussed in the introduction. Select several learning products (e.g., papers, essays, reports) that represent evidence of accomplishment of those purposes. If you have not previously done so, word process a one- to two-page reflective assessment of each learning product.

6.10 Word process a summary for your social work portfolio. Refer to Box 6.7 for an example. In your summary, be sure to demonstrate critical thinking and self-reflective abilities.

6.11 Sort through and determine which of the supportive documents you collected earlier should be included within the appendixes to the social work portfolio. Make your selections on the basis of the major purposes or expectations for the portfolio.

6.12 Compile all the materials within an attractive and professionally appealing form (e.g., expandable folder, extra large binder, or as an electronic presentation).

Collaborative Group Learning Exercises

6.13 Share your social work portfolio with your colleagues. Describe what you consider the strongest as well as the weakest aspects of your portfolio.

6.14 Ask one or more of your colleagues to make an objective, rigorous, and constructive evaluation of your portfolio. Request that they use relevant assessment criteria (e.g., those provided by your academic program or the general assessment rubric presented earlier in this chapter) to guide their evaluation. Make written notes of their feedback and consider the utility of the information for improving the quality of your portfolio.

6.15 Reflect back upon the processes you undertook to read and complete the exercises in this book. Share your observations and conclusions with your colleagues. Discuss what you gained and valued as well as those aspects you believe were insignificant or irrelevant. Describe what was difficult and what was easy. Share your overall impressions, particularly as they relate to the issues of lifelong learning and the utility of a social work portfolio.

6.16 Share your thoughts and feelings about the collaborative group aspects of this experience. Thank your colleagues and wish them well.

Portfolio Exercises

6.17 Use the results of your self-assessment and the input from your colleagues to further edit, revise, and improve the quality of your social work portfolio. Once completed, submit the final version to the intended recipient. As a social work student, you might submit the portfolio to your adviser, an instructor, the program director, or perhaps an assessment committee. Be sure to make backup copies of all your word-processed files and keep copies of those documents that might be difficult to replace.

6.18 When you receive feedback from the person or persons to whom you submitted your social work portfolio, consider the evaluative comments. Assess the relevance, accuracy, fairness, and utility of the information. Take what you view as constructive feedback and use it to improve the quality of your portfolio while keeping in mind that your next version may serve quite different purposes.

Optional Exercises

You have done so much work thus far in this book that it would simply be unreasonable to ask you to do any more. Therefore, we will not! Instead, consider the following exercises entirely optional. If you do choose to complete them, please do so after you have recovered from the exhausting process of completing your social work portfolio and all the exercises from previous chapters.

Throughout the course of this book, you completed several instruments. Some were online on the World Wide Web. Others were included in the Appendixes. You may find it helpful to see what your responses might be if you were to take a few of those instruments once again, now that some considerable amount of time has elapsed.

6.19 Go to Appendix 1 and complete the Lifelong Learning Questionnaire. Compare your score and your responses with those you made when you first completed the instrument. Reflect upon the results and consider whether you have become more or less of an active lifelong learner. Consider what factors may have contributed to the change.

6.20 Go to Appendix 4 to complete The Self-Assessment of Social Work Knowledge Survey. Compare your responses with those from the time you took the survey quite a while ago. In what areas do you now believe that you are more proficient than you were before? In what areas might you be less proficient? Reflect upon the implications of any changes that might be reflected in your responses.

6.21 Consider the other instruments included within the Appendixes along with those you completed online. If you wish, retake those to determine what changes, if any, may have occurred since the first time you completed them. Reflect upon the results and use the information to guide your efforts toward further lifelong learning.

Appendix 1
Lifelong Learning Questionnaire

The Lifelong Learning Questionnaire[1] (LLQ) may help you to consider various aspects of yourself as a lifelong learner. There are no right or wrong answers. Rather, the questionnaire may be used to stimulate reflection about your "learning self." Therefore, please consider your results as hypotheses to examine in the context of evidence from other sources.

Please read the following statements. Indicate your degree of agreement or disagreement with each statement by using the following codes:

1 = Strongly Agree

2 = Agree

3 = Disagree

4 = Strongly Disagree

_____ 1. I regularly read professional journals in my field.

_____ 2. I genuinely enjoy learning.

_____ 3. I always do more than the minimum requirements in courses, seminars, or workshops.

_____ 4. I regularly pursue opportunities to advance my knowledge and expertise.

_____ 5. I never become defensive when someone offers feedback that could improve my knowledge and skill.

_____ 6. I like to study.

_____ 7. I know my personal learning style.

_____ 8. I am actively involved in learning experiences.

_____ 9. I take personal responsibility for my own learning.

_____ 10. I view examinations as a way to learn.

_____ 11. I know how to conduct a professional literature review.

_____ 12. I sometimes contact national and international experts in my learning efforts.

_____ 13. I have a list of learning goals.

_____ 14. I have specific plans to advance my learning.

_____ 15. I enjoy teaching others.

_____ LLQ Score

---

[1] Preliminary draft of the Lifelong Learning Questionnaire. Copyright © 1999 by Barry R. Cournoyer. Reprinted by permission.

The Lifelong Learning Questionnaire is scored by adding your ratings to each of the 15 items. The sum represents your LLQ score. Scores between 15 and 60 are possible. Lower scores indicate greater strength in lifelong learning. Although we are still developing the Lifelong Learning Questionnaire, you may wish to consider your score in relation to the average score of a convenience sample of social work students. Twenty-one members of a first-year MSW practice class completed the LLQ in January 1999. They reflected an average score of 33.10 (range 20–43; SD 7.44) (Cournoyer, 1999).

Appendix 2
Common Phases of a
Professional Social Work Career

Social workers and social work students are usually quite familiar with various theories and models of human behavior and development. Indeed, the notion of "life span" or "life cycle" and terms such as "stages" and "phases" are often discussed in human behavior and the social environment (HBSE) courses and in social work practice courses as well. Many social workers can readily discuss various theories of individual, family, group, organizational, and community life-cycle development.

In particular, social workers may be quite knowledgeable about models of human development proposed by Erikson (1964, 1980), Maslow (1968), Havighurst (1953), Piaget (Evans, 1973), Kohlberg (Kohlberg, Levine, & Hewer, 1983), Gilligan (1982), and of course, Freud (1975).

General models of human development help social workers appreciate some of the issues people commonly confront at different stages of life. We may even extrapolate from them to identify certain common lifelong learning needs. However, when we consider the professional development of social workers, these models have modest applicability. The career paths of social workers often do not correlate directly with chronological age. Indeed, the stages of a typical career in social work tend to involve several other factors (Cohen, 1995) and may not proceed in a coherent sequence. Although many serve in direct practice positions for several years and then gradually assume increasing supervisory or administrative responsibilities, some social workers, perhaps because of previous experience, take management positions almost immediately following graduation. Others move into social policy or planning roles, and some gravitate to research-related positions. A few are interested in doctoral education, often to pursue an academic career in higher education, whereas others leave the profession entirely as they come to realize they are not personally able to deal with the extraordinary challenges of social service.

Many social workers move from one position to another and from one area of interest to others because of budgetary cutbacks, programmatic changes, or family relocation. Often, the phases of professional development or the tasks and functions within them occur in jumps and starts in no apparent sequence. Indeed, for many social workers, life tasks are recycled several times as they pursue, undertake, and finally conclude their professional development.

Obviously, many social workers reflect distinct career paths. Nevertheless, to provide a conceptual structure, we tentatively propose an outline of common phases or processes of a typical social work career. In doing so, we fully recognize the limitations of this approach.

A. Preprofessional

1. Explore, identify, learn about, and consider various vocational and professional career options
2. Become especially interested in social work and feel an affinity for the profession
3. Carefully and comprehensively examine the goodness-of-fit between the values of the profession and personal goals and aspirations
4. Select social work as a career choice; seek admission to and enroll in an educational program that leads to a professional degree

B. Academic

1. Develop knowledge and skills necessary to succeed as a social work student
2. Test the decision to pursue a career in social work and the goodness-of-fit between personal characteristics and professional social work values
3. Make a commitment to the profession of social work and its values and establish a professional identity
4. Develop broad-based, generic, or generalist knowledge and skills needed by all social workers
5. Select one or more areas of special interest within the broad scope of social work and develop special knowledge and skills for service within the area(s)
6. Begin the process of searching for a job or more advanced formal education (e.g., M.S.W., D.S.W., or Ph.D.)
7. Graduate from the university with a social work degree

C. Early Professional

1. Become licensed or certified as a social worker
2. Secure employment as a social worker
3. Identify gaps in the knowledge or skills needed to perform competently in the job or position
4. Develop knowledge and skills necessary for competent performance in the job or position
5. Obtain and use professional social work supervision to maintain and improve competence
6. Identify and undertake continuing education and lifelong learning opportunities

D. Midcareer

1. Achieve an optimal degree of comfort in a professional social work position
2. Add depth and breadth to professional knowledge, values, and skills
3. Become a recognized authority in an area of interest or expertise
4. Serve as a supervisor, seminar or workshop leader, or educator
5. Share your expertise through written and spoken communication with others

E. Late Career

1. Serve as a mentor to early and midcareer social work professionals
2. Reflect upon, speak, and write about broader issues of importance to the profession as a whole

Appendix 3
Index of Learning Styles

The Index of Learning Styles[1] (ILS) may help you identify your preferred style of learning. There are no right or wrong answers, nor are there preferred styles. Rather, the questionnaire may be used to stimulate reflection about your "style of learning." Please consider your results as hypotheses to examine in the context of evidence from other sources.

Index of Learning Styles

Barbara A. Soloman
First-Year College
North Carolina State University
Raleigh, North Carolina 27695

Richard M. Felder
Department of Chemical Engineering
North Carolina State University
Raleigh, NC 27695

Directions

Circle "a" or "b" to indicate your answer to every question. Please choose only one answer for each question. If both "a" and "b" seem to apply to you, choose the one that applies more frequently.

1. I understand something better after I
    (a) try it out.
    (b) think it through.

2. I would rather be considered
    (a) realistic.
    (b) innovative.

---

[1] Preliminary version of the Index of Learning Styles. Copyright © 1998 Barbara A. Soloman and Richard M. Felder. Reprinted by permission of the authors.

3. When I think about what I did yesterday, I am most likely to get
   (a) a picture.
   (b) words.

4. I tend to
   (a) understand details of a subject but may be fuzzy about its overall structure.
   (b) understand the overall structure but may be fuzzy about details.

5. When I am learning something new, it helps me to
   (a) talk about it.
   (b) think about it.

6. If I were a teacher, I would rather teach a course
   (a) that deals with facts and real life situations.
   (b) that deals with ideas and theories.

7. I prefer to get new information in
   (a) pictures, diagrams, graphs, or maps.
   (b) written directions or verbal information.

8. Once I understand
   (a) all the parts, I understand the whole thing.
   (b) the whole thing, I see how the parts fit.

9. In a study group working on difficult material, I am more likely to
   (a) jump in and contribute ideas.
   (b) sit back and listen.

10. I find it easier
    (a) to learn facts.
    (b) to learn concepts.

11. In a book with lots of pictures and charts, I am likely to
    (a) look over the pictures and charts carefully.
    (b) focus on the written text.

12. When I solve math problems
    (a) I usually work my way to the solutions one step at a time.
    (b) I often just see the solutions but then have to struggle to figure out the steps to get to them.

13. In classes I have taken
    (a) I have usually gotten to know many of the students.
    (b) I have rarely gotten to know many of the students.

14. In reading nonfiction, I prefer
    (a) something that teaches me new facts or tells me how to do something.
    (b) something that gives me new ideas to think about.

15. I like teachers
    (a) who put a lot of diagrams on the board.
    (b) who spend a lot of time explaining.

16. When I'm analyzing a story or a novel
    (a) I think of the incidents and try to put them together to figure out the themes.
    (b) I just know what the themes are when I finish reading and then I have to go back and find the incidents that demonstrate them.

17. When I start a homework problem, I am more likely to
    (a) start working on the solution immediately.
    (b) try to fully understand the problem first.

18. I prefer the idea of
    (a) certainty.
    (b) theory.

19. I remember best
    (a) what I see.
    (b) what I hear.

20. It is more important to me that an instructor
    (a) lay out the material in clear sequential steps.
    (b) give me an overall picture and relate the material to other subjects.

21. I prefer to study
    (a) in a study group.
    (b) alone.

22. I am more likely to be considered
    (a) careful about the details of my work.
    (b) creative about how to do my work.

23. When I get directions to a new place, I prefer
    (a) a map.
    (b) written instructions.

24. I learn
    (a) at a fairly regular pace. If I study hard, I'll "get it."
    (b) in fits and starts. I'll be totally confused and then suddenly it all "clicks."

25. I would rather first
    (a) try things out.
    (b) think about how I'm going to do it.

26. When I am reading for enjoyment, I like writers to
    (a) clearly say what they mean.
    (b) say things in creative, interesting ways.

27. When I see a diagram or sketch in class, I am most likely to remember
    (a) the picture.
    (b) what the instructor said about it.

28. When considering a body of information, I am more likely to
    (a) focus on details and miss the big picture.
    (b) try to understand the big picture before getting into the details.

29. I more easily remember
    (a) something I have done.
    (b) something I have thought a lot about.

30. When I have to perform a task, I prefer to
    (a) master one way of doing it.
    (b) come up with new ways of doing it.

31. When someone is showing me data, I prefer
    (a) charts or graphs.
    (b) text summarizing the results.

32. When writing a paper, I am more likely to
    (a) work on (think about or write) the beginning of the paper and progress forward.
    (b) work on (think about or write) different parts of the paper and then order them.

33. When I have to work on a group project, I first want to
    (a) have "group brainstorming" where everyone contributes ideas.
    (b) brainstorm individually and then come together as a group to compare ideas.

34. I consider it higher praise to call someone
    (a) sensible.
    (b) imaginative.

35. When I meet people at a party, I am more likely to remember
    (a) what they looked like.
    (b) what they said about themselves.

36. When I am learning a new subject, I prefer to
    (a) stay focused on that subject, learning as much about it as I can.
    (b) try to make connections between that subject and related subjects.

37. I am more likely to be considered
    (a) outgoing.
    (b) reserved.

38. I prefer courses that emphasize
    (a) concrete material (facts, data).
    (b) abstract material (concepts, theories).

39. For entertainment, I would rather
    (a) watch television.
    (b) read a book.

40. Some teachers start their lectures with an outline of what they will cover. Such outlines are
    (a) somewhat helpful to me.
    (b) very helpful to me.

41. The idea of doing homework in groups, with one grade for the entire group,
    (a) appeals to me.
    (b) does not appeal to me.

42. When I am doing long calculations,
    (a) I tend to repeat all my steps and check my work carefully.
    (b) I find checking my work tiresome and have to force myself to do it.

43. I tend to picture places I have been
    (a) easily and fairly accurately.
    (b) with difficulty and without much detail.

44. When solving problems in a group, I would be more likely to
    (a) think of the steps in the solution process.
    (b) think of possible consequences or applications of the solution in a wide range of areas.

ILS Scoring Sheet

Put "1"s in the appropriate spaces in the table below (e.g., if you answered "a" to Question 3, put a "1" in Column "a" by Question 3).

Total the columns and write the totals in the indicated spaces.

For each of the four scales, subtract the smaller total from the larger one. Write the difference (1 to 11) and the letter (a or b) with the larger total.

For example, if under "ACT/REF" you had 4 "a" and 7 "b" responses, you would write "3b" on the bottom line under that heading (3 = 7 – 4, and the "b" total was the larger of the two.)*

ACT/REF			SEN/INT			VIS/VRB			SEQ/GLO		
Q	a	b	Q	a	b	Q	a	b	Q	a	b
1			2			3			4		
5			6			7			8		
9			10			11			12		
13			14			15			16		
17			18			19			20		
21			22			23			24		
25			26			27			28		
29			30			31			32		
33			34			35			36		
37			38			39			40		
41			42			43			44		

(continued on page 96)

Total (sum X's in each column)

ACT/REF		SEN/INT		VIS/VRB		SEQ/GLO	
a	b	a	b	a	b	a	b

(Larger − Smaller) + Letter of Larger (see below*)

Example: If you totaled 3 for a and 8 for b, you would enter 5b.

Once you have totaled your scores, place them on the following table to graphically reflect your learning style preferences on the active–reflective, sensory–intuitive, visual–verbal, and sequential–global dimensions.

LEARNING STYLES RESULTS

ACT   REF
   11   9   7   5   3   1   1   3   5   7   9   11
                                    ←——————→

SEN   INT
   11   9   7   5   3   1   1   3   5   7   9   11
                                    ←——————→

VIS   VRB
   11   9   7   5   3   1   1   3   5   7   9   11
                                    ←——————→

SEQ   GLO
   11   9   7   5   3   1   1   3   5   7   9   11
                                    ←——————→

- If your score on a scale is 1–3, you are fairly well balanced on the two dimensions of that scale.
- If your score on a scale is 5–7, you have a moderate preference for one dimension of the scale and will learn more easily in a teaching environment that favors that dimension.
- If your score on a scale is 9–11, you have a very strong preference for one dimension of the scale. You may have real difficulty learning in an environment that does not support that preference.

ACT = Active Learners	REF = Reflective Learners
SEN = Sensing Learners	INT = Intuitive Learners
VIS = Visual Learners	VRB = Verbal Learners
SEQ = Sequential Learners	GLO = Global Learners

Scale developed by Richard M. Felder and Barbara A. Soloman. Copyright © 1998.

Appendix 4
The Self-Assessment of Social Work Knowledge Survey

We have developed this self-assessment instrument from fundamental knowledge, values, and skills identified by three major social work sources: Association of Social Work Boards (ASWB), which sponsors the nationally standardized social work examinations, the Council on Social Work Education (CSWE), which accredits schools and departments of social work throughout the United States, and the National Association of Social Work (NASW), which is the largest association of professional social workers in the world.

Take a few minutes to complete the following subjective self-assessment of your knowledge, values, and expertise in the following content areas. Do so by rating each of the following items on a simple 0–4 scale where 0 = Minimal Level of Knowledge and Expertise, 1 = Modest Level of Knowledge and Expertise, 2 = Satisfactory Level of Knowledge and Expertise, 3 = Superior Level of Knowledge and Expertise, and 4 = Excellent Level of Knowledge and Expertise. At the high end of the continuum, an Excellent rating indicates that the individual can proficiently, consistently, and appropriately demonstrate all six levels of Bloom's taxonomy (i.e., remember, understand, apply, analyze, synthesize, and evaluate). At the low end, Minimal suggests that the person has limited proficiency on some or all levels.

1. I can identify, describe, discuss, analyze, and apply knowledge of human behavior and social environment (HBSE) theory and research in professional efforts to understand and serve individuals.

Minimal Knowledge & Expertise	Modest Knowledge & Expertise	Satisfactory Knowledge & Expertise	Superior Knowledge & Expertise	Excellent Knowledge & Expertise
0	1	2	3	4

2. I can identify, describe, discuss, analyze, and apply knowledge of human behavior and social environment (HBSE) theory and research in professional efforts to understand and serve couples and dyads.

Minimal Knowledge & Expertise	Modest Knowledge & Expertise	Satisfactory Knowledge & Expertise	Superior Knowledge & Expertise	Excellent Knowledge & Expertise
0	1	2	3	4

3. I can identify, describe, discuss, analyze, and apply knowledge of human behavior and social environment (HBSE) theory and research in professional efforts to understand and serve families.

Minimal Knowledge & Expertise	Modest Knowledge & Expertise	Satisfactory Knowledge & Expertise	Superior Knowledge & Expertise	Excellent Knowledge & Expertise
0	1	2	3	4

4. I can identify, describe, discuss, analyze, and apply knowledge of human behavior and social environment (HBSE) theory and research in professional efforts to understand and serve small groups.

Minimal Knowledge & Expertise	Modest Knowledge & Expertise	Satisfactory Knowledge & Expertise	Superior Knowledge & Expertise	Excellent Knowledge & Expertise
0	1	2	3	4

5. I can identify, describe, discuss, analyze, and apply knowledge of human behavior and social environment (HBSE) theory and research in professional efforts to understand and serve organizations.

Minimal Knowledge & Expertise	Modest Knowledge & Expertise	Satisfactory Knowledge & Expertise	Superior Knowledge & Expertise	Excellent Knowledge & Expertise
0	1	2	3	4

6. I can identify, describe, discuss, analyze, and apply knowledge of human behavior and social environment (HBSE) theory and research in professional efforts to understand and serve communities.

Minimal Knowledge & Expertise	Modest Knowledge & Expertise	Satisfactory Knowledge & Expertise	Superior Knowledge & Expertise	Excellent Knowledge & Expertise
0	1	2	3	4

7. I can identify, describe, discuss, analyze, and apply knowledge of developmental life cycles in professional efforts to understand and serve individuals.

Minimal Knowledge & Expertise	Modest Knowledge & Expertise	Satisfactory Knowledge & Expertise	Superior Knowledge & Expertise	Excellent Knowledge & Expertise
0	1	2	3	4

8. I can identify, describe, discuss, analyze, and apply knowledge of developmental life cycles in professional efforts to understand and serve couples and dyads.

Minimal Knowledge & Expertise	Modest Knowledge & Expertise	Satisfactory Knowledge & Expertise	Superior Knowledge & Expertise	Excellent Knowledge & Expertise
0	1	2	3	4

9. I can identify, describe, discuss, analyze, and apply knowledge of developmental life cycles in professional efforts to understand and serve families.

Minimal Knowledge & Expertise	Modest Knowledge & Expertise	Satisfactory Knowledge & Expertise	Superior Knowledge & Expertise	Excellent Knowledge & Expertise
0	1	2	3	4

10. I can identify, describe, discuss, analyze, and apply knowledge of developmental life cycles in professional efforts to understand and serve small groups.

Minimal Knowledge & Expertise	Modest Knowledge & Expertise	Satisfactory Knowledge & Expertise	Superior Knowledge & Expertise	Excellent Knowledge & Expertise
0	1	2	3	4

11. I can identify, describe, discuss, analyze, and apply knowledge of developmental life cycles in professional efforts to understand and serve organizations.

Minimal Knowledge & Expertise	Modest Knowledge & Expertise	Satisfactory Knowledge & Expertise	Superior Knowledge & Expertise	Excellent Knowledge & Expertise
0	1	2	3	4

12. I can identify, describe, discuss, analyze, and apply knowledge of developmental life cycles in professional efforts to understand and serve communities.

Minimal Knowledge & Expertise	Modest Knowledge & Expertise	Satisfactory Knowledge & Expertise	Superior Knowledge & Expertise	Excellent Knowledge & Expertise
0	1	2	3	4

13. I can identify, describe, discuss, analyze, and apply knowledge of abnormal and addictive phenomena in professional efforts to understand and serve individuals.

Minimal Knowledge & Expertise	Modest Knowledge & Expertise	Satisfactory Knowledge & Expertise	Superior Knowledge & Expertise	Excellent Knowledge & Expertise
0	1	2	3	4

14. I can identify, describe, discuss, analyze, and apply knowledge of abnormal and addictive phenomena in professional efforts to understand and serve families.

Minimal Knowledge & Expertise	Modest Knowledge & Expertise	Satisfactory Knowledge & Expertise	Superior Knowledge & Expertise	Excellent Knowledge & Expertise
0	1	2	3	4

15. I can identify, describe, discuss, analyze, and apply knowledge of abuse and neglect in professional efforts to understand and serve individuals victimized by such phenomena.

Minimal Knowledge & Expertise	Modest Knowledge & Expertise	Satisfactory Knowledge & Expertise	Superior Knowledge & Expertise	Excellent Knowledge & Expertise
0	1	2	3	4

16. I can identify, describe, discuss, analyze, and apply knowledge of abuse and neglect in professional efforts to understand and serve individuals who have or might engage in abusive or neglectful behavior toward others.

Minimal Knowledge & Expertise	Modest Knowledge & Expertise	Satisfactory Knowledge & Expertise	Superior Knowledge & Expertise	Excellent Knowledge & Expertise
0	1	2	3	4

17. I can identify, describe, discuss, analyze, and apply knowledge of abuse and neglect in professional efforts to understand and serve families affected by such phenomena.

Minimal Knowledge & Expertise	Modest Knowledge & Expertise	Satisfactory Knowledge & Expertise	Superior Knowledge & Expertise	Excellent Knowledge & Expertise
0	1	2	3	4

18. I can identify, describe, discuss, analyze, and apply knowledge of abuse and neglect in professional efforts to prevent or ameliorate the effects of such phenomena within communities.

Minimal Knowledge & Expertise	Modest Knowledge & Expertise	Satisfactory Knowledge & Expertise	Superior Knowledge & Expertise	Excellent Knowledge & Expertise
0	1	2	3	4

19. I can identify, describe, discuss, analyze, and apply knowledge of race, ethnicity, and culture in professional efforts to understand and serve clients.

Minimal Knowledge & Expertise	Modest Knowledge & Expertise	Satisfactory Knowledge & Expertise	Superior Knowledge & Expertise	Excellent Knowledge & Expertise
0	1	2	3	4

20. I can identify, describe, discuss, analyze, and apply knowledge of sexual orientation in professional efforts to understand and serve clients.

Minimal Knowledge & Expertise	Modest Knowledge & Expertise	Satisfactory Knowledge & Expertise	Superior Knowledge & Expertise	Excellent Knowledge & Expertise
0	1	2	3	4

21. I can identify, describe, discuss, analyze, and apply knowledge of sex and gender in professional efforts to understand and serve clients.

Minimal Knowledge & Expertise	Modest Knowledge & Expertise	Satisfactory Knowledge & Expertise	Superior Knowledge & Expertise	Excellent Knowledge & Expertise
0	1	2	3	4

22. I can identify, describe, discuss, analyze, and apply knowledge of diagnosis and assessment in social work practice with individuals.

Minimal Knowledge & Expertise	Modest Knowledge & Expertise	Satisfactory Knowledge & Expertise	Superior Knowledge & Expertise	Excellent Knowledge & Expertise
0	1	2	3	4

23. I can identify, describe, discuss, analyze, and apply knowledge of diagnosis and assessment in social work practice with couples and dyads.

Minimal Knowledge & Expertise	Modest Knowledge & Expertise	Satisfactory Knowledge & Expertise	Superior Knowledge & Expertise	Excellent Knowledge & Expertise
0	1	2	3	4

24. I can identify, describe, discuss, analyze, and apply knowledge of diagnosis and assessment in social work practice with families.

Minimal Knowledge & Expertise	Modest Knowledge & Expertise	Satisfactory Knowledge & Expertise	Superior Knowledge & Expertise	Excellent Knowledge & Expertise
0	1	2	3	4

25. I can identify, describe, discuss, analyze, and apply knowledge of diagnosis and assessment in social work practice with small groups.

Minimal Knowledge & Expertise	Modest Knowledge & Expertise	Satisfactory Knowledge & Expertise	Superior Knowledge & Expertise	Excellent Knowledge & Expertise
0	1	2	3	4

26. I can identify, describe, discuss, analyze, and apply knowledge of diagnosis and assessment in social work practice with organizations.

Minimal Knowledge & Expertise	Modest Knowledge & Expertise	Satisfactory Knowledge & Expertise	Superior Knowledge & Expertise	Excellent Knowledge & Expertise
0	1	2	3	4

27. I can identify, describe, discuss, analyze, and apply knowledge of diagnosis and assessment in social work practice with communities.

Minimal Knowledge & Expertise	Modest Knowledge & Expertise	Satisfactory Knowledge & Expertise	Superior Knowledge & Expertise	Excellent Knowledge & Expertise
0	1	2	3	4

28. I can identify, describe, discuss, analyze, and apply knowledge of psychosocial history taking and data collection process in professional efforts to understand and serve individuals.

Minimal Knowledge & Expertise	Modest Knowledge & Expertise	Satisfactory Knowledge & Expertise	Superior Knowledge & Expertise	Excellent Knowledge & Expertise
0	1	2	3	4

29. I can identify, describe, discuss, analyze, and apply knowledge of psychosocial history taking and data collection process in professional efforts to understand and serve couples and dyads.

Minimal Knowledge & Expertise	Modest Knowledge & Expertise	Satisfactory Knowledge & Expertise	Superior Knowledge & Expertise	Excellent Knowledge & Expertise
0	1	2	3	4

30. I can identify, describe, discuss, analyze, and apply knowledge of psychosocial history taking and data collection process in professional efforts to understand and serve families.

Minimal Knowledge & Expertise	Modest Knowledge & Expertise	Satisfactory Knowledge & Expertise	Superior Knowledge & Expertise	Excellent Knowledge & Expertise
0	1	2	3	4

31. I can identify, describe, discuss, analyze, and apply knowledge of psychosocial history taking and data collection process in professional efforts to understand and serve small groups.

Minimal Knowledge & Expertise	Modest Knowledge & Expertise	Satisfactory Knowledge & Expertise	Superior Knowledge & Expertise	Excellent Knowledge & Expertise
0	1	2	3	4

32. I can identify, describe, discuss, analyze, and apply knowledge of psychosocial history taking and data collection process in professional efforts to understand and serve organizations.

Minimal Knowledge & Expertise	Modest Knowledge & Expertise	Satisfactory Knowledge & Expertise	Superior Knowledge & Expertise	Excellent Knowledge & Expertise
0	1	2	3	4

33. I can identify, describe, discuss, analyze, and apply knowledge of psychosocial history taking and data collection process in professional efforts to understand and serve communities.

Minimal Knowledge & Expertise	Modest Knowledge & Expertise	Satisfactory Knowledge & Expertise	Superior Knowledge & Expertise	Excellent Knowledge & Expertise
0	1	2	3	4

34. I can identify, describe, discuss, analyze, and apply knowledge of psychosocial assessment instruments in professional efforts to understand and serve individuals.

Minimal Knowledge & Expertise	Modest Knowledge & Expertise	Satisfactory Knowledge & Expertise	Superior Knowledge & Expertise	Excellent Knowledge & Expertise
0	1	2	3	4

35. I can identify, describe, discuss, analyze, and apply knowledge of psychosocial assessment instruments in professional efforts to understand and serve couples and dyads.

Minimal Knowledge & Expertise	Modest Knowledge & Expertise	Satisfactory Knowledge & Expertise	Superior Knowledge & Expertise	Excellent Knowledge & Expertise
0	1	2	3	4

36. I can identify, describe, discuss, analyze, and apply knowledge of psychosocial assessment instruments in professional efforts to understand and serve families.

Minimal Knowledge & Expertise	Modest Knowledge & Expertise	Satisfactory Knowledge & Expertise	Superior Knowledge & Expertise	Excellent Knowledge & Expertise
0	1	2	3	4

37. I can identify, describe, discuss, analyze, and apply knowledge of psychosocial assessment instruments in professional efforts to understand and serve small groups.

Minimal Knowledge & Expertise	Modest Knowledge & Expertise	Satisfactory Knowledge & Expertise	Superior Knowledge & Expertise	Excellent Knowledge & Expertise
0	1	2	3	4

38. I can identify, describe, discuss, analyze, and apply knowledge of psychosocial assessment instruments in professional efforts to understand and serve organizations.

Minimal Knowledge & Expertise	Modest Knowledge & Expertise	Satisfactory Knowledge & Expertise	Superior Knowledge & Expertise	Excellent Knowledge & Expertise
0	1	2	3	4

39. I can identify, describe, discuss, analyze, and apply knowledge of psychosocial assessment instruments in professional efforts to understand and serve communities.

Minimal Knowledge & Expertise	Modest Knowledge & Expertise	Satisfactory Knowledge & Expertise	Superior Knowledge & Expertise	Excellent Knowledge & Expertise
0	1	2	3	4

40. I can identify, describe, discuss, analyze, and apply knowledge of problem identification and goal definition in professional efforts to understand and serve individuals.

Minimal Knowledge & Expertise	Modest Knowledge & Expertise	Satisfactory Knowledge & Expertise	Superior Knowledge & Expertise	Excellent Knowledge & Expertise
0	1	2	3	4

41. I can identify, describe, discuss, analyze, and apply knowledge of problem identification and goal definition in professional efforts to understand and serve couples and dyads.

Minimal Knowledge & Expertise	Modest Knowledge & Expertise	Satisfactory Knowledge & Expertise	Superior Knowledge & Expertise	Excellent Knowledge & Expertise
0	1	2	3	4

42. I can identify, describe, discuss, analyze, and apply knowledge of problem identification and goal definition in professional efforts to understand and serve families.

Minimal Knowledge & Expertise	Modest Knowledge & Expertise	Satisfactory Knowledge & Expertise	Superior Knowledge & Expertise	Excellent Knowledge & Expertise
0	1	2	3	4

43. I can identify, describe, discuss, analyze, and apply knowledge of problem identification and goal definition in professional efforts to understand and serve small groups.

Minimal Knowledge & Expertise	Modest Knowledge & Expertise	Satisfactory Knowledge & Expertise	Superior Knowledge & Expertise	Excellent Knowledge & Expertise
0	1	2	3	4

44. I can identify, describe, discuss, analyze, and apply knowledge of problem identification and goal definition in professional efforts to understand and serve organizations.

Minimal Knowledge & Expertise	Modest Knowledge & Expertise	Satisfactory Knowledge & Expertise	Superior Knowledge & Expertise	Excellent Knowledge & Expertise
0	1	2	3	4

45. I can identify, describe, discuss, analyze, and apply knowledge of problem identification and goal definition in professional efforts to understand and serve communities.

Minimal Knowledge & Expertise	Modest Knowledge & Expertise	Satisfactory Knowledge & Expertise	Superior Knowledge & Expertise	Excellent Knowledge & Expertise
0	1	2	3	4

46. I can identify, describe, discuss, analyze, and apply knowledge related to the identification and assessment of strengths, assets, and capacities in professional efforts to understand and serve individuals.

Minimal Knowledge & Expertise	Modest Knowledge & Expertise	Satisfactory Knowledge & Expertise	Superior Knowledge & Expertise	Excellent Knowledge & Expertise
0	1	2	3	4

47. I can identify, describe, discuss, analyze, and apply knowledge related to the identification and assessment of strengths, assets, and capacities in professional efforts to understand and serve couples and dyads.

Minimal Knowledge & Expertise	Modest Knowledge & Expertise	Satisfactory Knowledge & Expertise	Superior Knowledge & Expertise	Excellent Knowledge & Expertise
0	1	2	3	4

48. I can identify, describe, discuss, analyze, and apply knowledge related to the identification and assessment of strengths, assets, and capacities in professional efforts to understand and serve families.

Minimal Knowledge & Expertise	Modest Knowledge & Expertise	Satisfactory Knowledge & Expertise	Superior Knowledge & Expertise	Excellent Knowledge & Expertise
0	1	2	3	4

49. I can identify, describe, discuss, analyze, and apply knowledge related to the identification and assessment of strengths, assets, and capacities in professional efforts to understand and serve small groups.

Minimal Knowledge & Expertise	Modest Knowledge & Expertise	Satisfactory Knowledge & Expertise	Superior Knowledge & Expertise	Excellent Knowledge & Expertise
0	1	2	3	4

50. I can identify, describe, discuss, analyze, and apply knowledge related to the identification and assessment of strengths, assets, and capacities in professional efforts to understand and serve organizations.

Minimal Knowledge & Expertise	Modest Knowledge & Expertise	Satisfactory Knowledge & Expertise	Superior Knowledge & Expertise	Excellent Knowledge & Expertise
0	1	2	3	4

51. I can identify, describe, discuss, analyze, and apply knowledge related to the identification and assessment of strengths, assets, and capacities in professional efforts to understand and serve communities.

Minimal Knowledge & Expertise	Modest Knowledge & Expertise	Satisfactory Knowledge & Expertise	Superior Knowledge & Expertise	Excellent Knowledge & Expertise
0	1	2	3	4

52. I can identify, describe, discuss, analyze, and apply knowledge of mental and behavioral disorders in professional efforts to understand and serve individuals.

Minimal Knowledge & Expertise	Modest Knowledge & Expertise	Satisfactory Knowledge & Expertise	Superior Knowledge & Expertise	Excellent Knowledge & Expertise
0	1	2	3	4

53. I can identify, describe, discuss, analyze, and apply knowledge of mental and behavioral disorders in professional efforts to understand and serve couples and dyads.

Minimal Knowledge & Expertise	Modest Knowledge & Expertise	Satisfactory Knowledge & Expertise	Superior Knowledge & Expertise	Excellent Knowledge & Expertise
0	1	2	3	4

54. I can identify, describe, discuss, analyze, and apply knowledge of mental and behavioral disorders in professional efforts to understand and serve families.

Minimal Knowledge & Expertise	Modest Knowledge & Expertise	Satisfactory Knowledge & Expertise	Superior Knowledge & Expertise	Excellent Knowledge & Expertise
0	1	2	3	4

55. I can identify, describe, discuss, analyze, and apply knowledge of mental and behavioral disorders in professional efforts to understand and serve small groups.

Minimal Knowledge & Expertise	Modest Knowledge & Expertise	Satisfactory Knowledge & Expertise	Superior Knowledge & Expertise	Excellent Knowledge & Expertise
0	1	2	3	4

56. I can identify, describe, discuss, analyze, and apply knowledge of mental and behavioral disorders in professional efforts to understand and serve organizations.

Minimal Knowledge & Expertise	Modest Knowledge & Expertise	Satisfactory Knowledge & Expertise	Superior Knowledge & Expertise	Excellent Knowledge & Expertise
0	1	2	3	4

57. I can identify, describe, discuss, analyze, and apply knowledge of mental and behavioral disorders in professional efforts to understand and serve communities.

Minimal Knowledge & Expertise	Modest Knowledge & Expertise	Satisfactory Knowledge & Expertise	Superior Knowledge & Expertise	Excellent Knowledge & Expertise
0	1	2	3	4

58. I can identify, describe, discuss, analyze, and apply knowledge related to the assessment of a person's risk of harming her- or himself or others in professional efforts to understand and serve clients.

Minimal Knowledge & Expertise	Modest Knowledge & Expertise	Satisfactory Knowledge & Expertise	Superior Knowledge & Expertise	Excellent Knowledge & Expertise
0	1	2	3	4

59. I can identify, describe, discuss, analyze, and apply knowledge of the current version of the American Psychiatric Association's *Diagnostic and Statistical Manual* in professional efforts to understand and serve clients.

Minimal Knowledge & Expertise	Modest Knowledge & Expertise	Satisfactory Knowledge & Expertise	Superior Knowledge & Expertise	Excellent Knowledge & Expertise
0	1	2	3	4

60. I can identify, describe, discuss, analyze, and apply knowledge of the effects of the environment upon people in professional efforts to understand and serve clients.

Minimal Knowledge & Expertise	Modest Knowledge & Expertise	Satisfactory Knowledge & Expertise	Superior Knowledge & Expertise	Excellent Knowledge & Expertise
0	1	2	3	4

61. I can identify, describe, discuss, analyze, and apply knowledge of the elements of intervention processes in professional efforts to understand and serve individuals.

Minimal Knowledge & Expertise	Modest Knowledge & Expertise	Satisfactory Knowledge & Expertise	Superior Knowledge & Expertise	Excellent Knowledge & Expertise
0	1	2	3	4

62. I can identify, describe, discuss, analyze, and apply knowledge of the elements of intervention processes in professional efforts to understand and serve couples and dyads.

Minimal Knowledge & Expertise	Modest Knowledge & Expertise	Satisfactory Knowledge & Expertise	Superior Knowledge & Expertise	Excellent Knowledge & Expertise
0	1	2	3	4

63. I can identify, describe, discuss, analyze, and apply knowledge of the elements of intervention processes in professional efforts to understand and serve families.

Minimal Knowledge & Expertise	Modest Knowledge & Expertise	Satisfactory Knowledge & Expertise	Superior Knowledge & Expertise	Excellent Knowledge & Expertise
0	1	2	3	4

64. I can identify, describe, discuss, analyze, and apply knowledge of the elements of intervention processes in professional efforts to understand and serve small groups.

Minimal Knowledge & Expertise	Modest Knowledge & Expertise	Satisfactory Knowledge & Expertise	Superior Knowledge & Expertise	Excellent Knowledge & Expertise
0	1	2	3	4

65. I can identify, describe, discuss, analyze, and apply knowledge of the elements of the intervention process in professional efforts to understand and serve organizations.

Minimal Knowledge & Expertise	Modest Knowledge & Expertise	Satisfactory Knowledge & Expertise	Superior Knowledge & Expertise	Excellent Knowledge & Expertise
0	1	2	3	4

66. I can identify, describe, discuss, analyze, and apply knowledge of the elements of intervention processes in professional efforts to understand and serve communities.

Minimal Knowledge & Expertise	Modest Knowledge & Expertise	Satisfactory Knowledge & Expertise	Superior Knowledge & Expertise	Excellent Knowledge & Expertise
0	1	2	3	4

67. I can identify, describe, discuss, analyze, and apply knowledge of at least two theoretical models of social work practice, counseling, and psychotherapy in professional efforts to understand and serve individuals.

Minimal Knowledge & Expertise	Modest Knowledge & Expertise	Satisfactory Knowledge & Expertise	Superior Knowledge & Expertise	Excellent Knowledge & Expertise
0	1	2	3	4

68. I can identify, describe, discuss, analyze, and apply knowledge of at least two theoretical models of social work practice, counseling, and psychotherapy in professional efforts to understand and serve couples and dyads.

Minimal Knowledge & Expertise	Modest Knowledge & Expertise	Satisfactory Knowledge & Expertise	Superior Knowledge & Expertise	Excellent Knowledge & Expertise
0	1	2	3	4

69. I can identify, describe, discuss, analyze, and apply knowledge of at least two theoretical models of social work practice, counseling, and psychotherapy in professional efforts to understand and serve families.

Minimal Knowledge & Expertise	Modest Knowledge & Expertise	Satisfactory Knowledge & Expertise	Superior Knowledge & Expertise	Excellent Knowledge & Expertise
0	1	2	3	4

70. I can identify, describe, discuss, analyze, and apply knowledge of at least two theoretical models of social work practice, counseling, and psychotherapy in professional efforts to understand and serve small groups.

Minimal Knowledge & Expertise	Modest Knowledge & Expertise	Satisfactory Knowledge & Expertise	Superior Knowledge & Expertise	Excellent Knowledge & Expertise
0	1	2	3	4

71. I can identify, describe, discuss, analyze, and apply knowledge of theoretical models of prevention and intervention in professional efforts to understand and serve organizations.

Minimal Knowledge & Expertise	Modest Knowledge & Expertise	Satisfactory Knowledge & Expertise	Superior Knowledge & Expertise	Excellent Knowledge & Expertise
0	1	2	3	4

72. I can identify, describe, discuss, analyze, and apply knowledge of theoretical models of prevention and intervention in professional efforts to understand and serve communities.

Minimal Knowledge & Expertise	Modest Knowledge & Expertise	Satisfactory Knowledge & Expertise	Superior Knowledge & Expertise	Excellent Knowledge & Expertise
0	1	2	3	4

73. I can identify, describe, discuss, analyze, and apply knowledge of several strategies and techniques in professional efforts to prevent the occurrence of at least one social problem.

Minimal Knowledge & Expertise	Modest Knowledge & Expertise	Satisfactory Knowledge & Expertise	Superior Knowledge & Expertise	Excellent Knowledge & Expertise
0	1	2	3	4

74. I can identify, describe, discuss, analyze, and apply knowledge of several strategies and techniques in professional efforts to intervene with clients affected by at least one social problem.

Minimal Knowledge & Expertise	Modest Knowledge & Expertise	Satisfactory Knowledge & Expertise	Superior Knowledge & Expertise	Excellent Knowledge & Expertise
0	1	2	3	4

75. I can identify, describe, discuss, analyze, and apply knowledge of professional services to at least two target populations (e.g., members of a racial or ethnic minority group, inner city youth, persons affected by physical or emotional disability).

Minimal Knowledge & Expertise	Modest Knowledge & Expertise	Satisfactory Knowledge & Expertise	Superior Knowledge & Expertise	Excellent Knowledge & Expertise
0	1	2	3	4

76. I can identify, describe, discuss, analyze, and apply knowledge of interviewing skills and techniques in professional efforts to understand and serve individuals.

Minimal Knowledge & Expertise	Modest Knowledge & Expertise	Satisfactory Knowledge & Expertise	Superior Knowledge & Expertise	Excellent Knowledge & Expertise
0	1	2	3	4

77. I can identify, describe, discuss, analyze, and apply knowledge of interviewing skills and techniques in professional efforts to understand and serve couples and dyads.

Minimal Knowledge & Expertise	Modest Knowledge & Expertise	Satisfactory Knowledge & Expertise	Superior Knowledge & Expertise	Excellent Knowledge & Expertise
0	1	2	3	4

78. I can identify, describe, discuss, analyze, and apply knowledge of interviewing skills and techniques in professional efforts to understand and serve families.

Minimal Knowledge & Expertise	Modest Knowledge & Expertise	Satisfactory Knowledge & Expertise	Superior Knowledge & Expertise	Excellent Knowledge & Expertise
0	1	2	3	4

79. I can identify, describe, discuss, analyze, and apply knowledge of interviewing skills and techniques in professional efforts to understand and serve small groups.

Minimal Knowledge & Expertise	Modest Knowledge & Expertise	Satisfactory Knowledge & Expertise	Superior Knowledge & Expertise	Excellent Knowledge & Expertise
0	1	2	3	4

80. I can identify, describe, discuss, analyze, and apply knowledge of interviewing skills and techniques in professional efforts to understand and serve organizations.

Minimal Knowledge & Expertise	Modest Knowledge & Expertise	Satisfactory Knowledge & Expertise	Superior Knowledge & Expertise	Excellent Knowledge & Expertise
0	1	2	3	4

81. I can identify, describe, discuss, analyze, and apply knowledge of interviewing skills and techniques in professional efforts to understand and serve communities.

Minimal Knowledge & Expertise	Modest Knowledge & Expertise	Satisfactory Knowledge & Expertise	Superior Knowledge & Expertise	Excellent Knowledge & Expertise
0	1	2	3	4

82. I can identify, describe, discuss, analyze, and apply knowledge related to the evaluation of progress in social work practice in professional efforts to serve individuals.

Minimal Knowledge & Expertise	Modest Knowledge & Expertise	Satisfactory Knowledge & Expertise	Superior Knowledge & Expertise	Excellent Knowledge & Expertise
0	1	2	3	4

83. I can identify, describe, discuss, analyze, and apply knowledge related to the evaluation of progress in social work practice in professional efforts to serve couples and dyads.

Minimal Knowledge & Expertise	Modest Knowledge & Expertise	Satisfactory Knowledge & Expertise	Superior Knowledge & Expertise	Excellent Knowledge & Expertise
0	1	2	3	4

84. I can identify, describe, discuss, analyze, and apply knowledge related to the evaluation of progress in social work practice in professional efforts to serve families.

Minimal Knowledge & Expertise	Modest Knowledge & Expertise	Satisfactory Knowledge & Expertise	Superior Knowledge & Expertise	Excellent Knowledge & Expertise
0	1	2	3	4

85. I can identify, describe, discuss, analyze, and apply knowledge related to the evaluation of progress in social work practice in professional efforts to serve small groups.

Minimal Knowledge & Expertise	Modest Knowledge & Expertise	Satisfactory Knowledge & Expertise	Superior Knowledge & Expertise	Excellent Knowledge & Expertise
0	1	2	3	4

86. I can identify, describe, discuss, analyze, and apply knowledge related to the evaluation of progress in social work practice in professional efforts to serve organizations.

Minimal Knowledge & Expertise	Modest Knowledge & Expertise	Satisfactory Knowledge & Expertise	Superior Knowledge & Expertise	Excellent Knowledge & Expertise
0	1	2	3	4

87. I can identify, describe, discuss, analyze, and apply knowledge related to the evaluation of progress in social work practice in professional efforts to serve communities.

Minimal Knowledge & Expertise	Modest Knowledge & Expertise	Satisfactory Knowledge & Expertise	Superior Knowledge & Expertise	Excellent Knowledge & Expertise
0	1	2	3	4

88. I can identify, describe, discuss, analyze, and apply knowledge related to the selection and use of prevention, intervention, or treatment strategies and techniques in professional service to individuals.

Minimal Knowledge & Expertise	Modest Knowledge & Expertise	Satisfactory Knowledge & Expertise	Superior Knowledge & Expertise	Excellent Knowledge & Expertise
0	1	2	3	4

89. I can identify, describe, discuss, analyze, and apply knowledge related to the selection and use of prevention, intervention, or treatment strategies and techniques in professional service to couples and dyads.

Minimal Knowledge & Expertise	Modest Knowledge & Expertise	Satisfactory Knowledge & Expertise	Superior Knowledge & Expertise	Excellent Knowledge & Expertise
0	1	2	3	4

90. I can identify, describe, discuss, analyze, and apply knowledge related to the selection and use of prevention, intervention, or treatment strategies and techniques in professional service to families.

Minimal Knowledge & Expertise	Modest Knowledge & Expertise	Satisfactory Knowledge & Expertise	Superior Knowledge & Expertise	Excellent Knowledge & Expertise
0	1	2	3	4

91. I can identify, describe, discuss, analyze, and apply knowledge related to the selection and use of prevention, intervention, or treatment strategies and techniques in professional service to small groups.

Minimal Knowledge & Expertise	Modest Knowledge & Expertise	Satisfactory Knowledge & Expertise	Superior Knowledge & Expertise	Excellent Knowledge & Expertise
0	1	2	3	4

92. I can identify, describe, discuss, analyze, and apply knowledge related to the selection and use of prevention or intervention strategies and techniques in professional service to organizations.

Minimal Knowledge & Expertise	Modest Knowledge & Expertise	Satisfactory Knowledge & Expertise	Superior Knowledge & Expertise	Excellent Knowledge & Expertise
0	1	2	3	4

93. I can identify, describe, discuss, analyze, and apply knowledge related to the selection and use of prevention or intervention strategies and techniques in professional service to communities.

Minimal Knowledge & Expertise	Modest Knowledge & Expertise	Satisfactory Knowledge & Expertise	Superior Knowledge & Expertise	Excellent Knowledge & Expertise
0	1	2	3	4

94. I can identify, describe, discuss, analyze, and apply knowledge related to the professional use of self in social work practice.

Minimal Knowledge & Expertise	Modest Knowledge & Expertise	Satisfactory Knowledge & Expertise	Superior Knowledge & Expertise	Excellent Knowledge & Expertise
0	1	2	3	4

95. I can identify, describe, discuss, analyze, and apply knowledge related to interdisciplinary relationships as they affect professional efforts to understand and serve clients.

Minimal Knowledge & Expertise	Modest Knowledge & Expertise	Satisfactory Knowledge & Expertise	Superior Knowledge & Expertise	Excellent Knowledge & Expertise
0	1	2	3	4

96. I can identify, describe, discuss, analyze, and apply knowledge of theories, principles, and techniques of interpersonal communication in professional efforts to understand and serve clients.

Minimal Knowledge & Expertise	Modest Knowledge & Expertise	Satisfactory Knowledge & Expertise	Superior Knowledge & Expertise	Excellent Knowledge & Expertise
0	1	2	3	4

97. I can identify, describe, discuss, analyze, and apply knowledge related to the development and use of the professional social worker-client relationship in professional efforts to understand and serve clients

Minimal Knowledge & Expertise	Modest Knowledge & Expertise	Satisfactory Knowledge & Expertise	Superior Knowledge & Expertise	Excellent Knowledge & Expertise
0	1	2	3	4

98. I can identify, describe, discuss, analyze, and apply knowledge of professional values and ethics in providing social work services.

Minimal Knowledge & Expertise	Modest Knowledge & Expertise	Satisfactory Knowledge & Expertise	Superior Knowledge & Expertise	Excellent Knowledge & Expertise
0	1	2	3	4

99. I can identify, describe, discuss, analyze, and apply knowledge related to supervision and supervisory processes in professional contexts.

Minimal Knowledge & Expertise	Modest Knowledge & Expertise	Satisfactory Knowledge & Expertise	Superior Knowledge & Expertise	Excellent Knowledge & Expertise
0	1	2	3	4

100. I can identify, describe, discuss, analyze, and apply knowledge related to research methods, processes, and outcomes in professional social work service.

Minimal Knowledge & Expertise	Modest Knowledge & Expertise	Satisfactory Knowledge & Expertise	Superior Knowledge & Expertise	Excellent Knowledge & Expertise
0	1	2	3	4

101. I can identify, describe, discuss, analyze, and apply knowledge of at least two major social policies for professional service.

Minimal Knowledge & Expertise	Modest Knowledge & Expertise	Satisfactory Knowledge & Expertise	Superior Knowledge & Expertise	Excellent Knowledge & Expertise
0	1	2	3	4

102. I can engage in policy analysis for professional service.

Minimal Knowledge & Expertise	Modest Knowledge & Expertise	Satisfactory Knowledge & Expertise	Superior Knowledge & Expertise	Excellent Knowledge & Expertise
0	1	2	3	4

103. I can engage in policy development for professional service.

Minimal Knowledge & Expertise	Modest Knowledge & Expertise	Satisfactory Knowledge & Expertise	Superior Knowledge & Expertise	Excellent Knowledge & Expertise
0	1	2	3	4

104. I can identify, describe, discuss, analyze, and apply knowledge of personnel management and administration for professional service.

Minimal Knowledge & Expertise	Modest Knowledge & Expertise	Satisfactory Knowledge & Expertise	Superior Knowledge & Expertise	Excellent Knowledge & Expertise
0	1	2	3	4

105. I can identify, describe, discuss, analyze, and apply knowledge of program management and administration for professional service.

Minimal Knowledge & Expertise	Modest Knowledge & Expertise	Satisfactory Knowledge & Expertise	Superior Knowledge & Expertise	Excellent Knowledge & Expertise
0	1	2	3	4

Appendix 5
The Social Work Interests Instrument [1]

Review the United States Bureau of Labor social work job descriptions presented in Chapter 4. Then indicate your current level of interest in each social work position by circling the number that best reflects your preference. Since this is not an exhaustive list, you may add other social work positions. You may also find it useful to refer back to this instrument periodically throughout your social work career. Your interests could change from time to time.

SOCIAL WORK INTERESTS INSTRUMENT

Clinical	1	2	3	4	5
Social Worker	No Interest	Little Interest	Some Interest	Mild Interest	Strong Interest
Child Welfare or Family					
Services	1	2	3	4	5
Social Worker	No Interest	Little Interest	Some Interest	Mild Interest	Strong Interest
Child or Adult Protection					
Services	1	2	3	4	5
Social Worker	No Interest	Little Interest	Some Interest	Mild Interest	Strong Interest
Mental-Health	1	2	3	4	5
Social Worker	No Interest	Little Interest	Some Interest	Mild Interest	Strong Interest
Health Care	1	2	3	4	5
Social Worker	No Interest	Little Interest	Some Interest	Mild Interest	Strong Interest
School	1	2	3	4	5
Social Worker	No Interest	Little Interest	Some Interest	Mild Interest	Strong Interest
Criminal Justice	1	2	3	4	5
Social Worker	No Interest	Little Interest	Some Interest	Mild Interest	Strong Interest
Occupational	1	2	3	4	5
Social Worker	No Interest	Little Interest	Some Interest	Mild Interest	Strong Interest
Gerontology	1	2	3	4	5
Social Worker	No Interest	Little Interest	Some Interest	Mild Interest	Strong Interest
Social Work	1	2	3	4	5
Administrator	No Interest	Little Interest	Some Interest	Mild Interest	Strong Interest
Social Work					
Planner and	1	2	3	4	5
Policy Maker	No Interest	Little Interest	Some Interest	Mild Interest	Strong Interest
	1	2	3	4	5
_____	No Interest	Little Interest	Some Interest	Mild Interest	Strong Interest
	1	2	3	4	5
_____	No Interest	Little Interest	Some Interest	Mild Interest	Strong Interest

[1] We created this little instrument based on the social work jobs described by the United States Bureau of Labor Statistics.

Appendix 6
Sample Cover Letter

Maria Sanchez, B.S.W. Student
192107 Alimingo Ave., Apt. 12B
Indianapolis, IN 46260
(317) 274-0001

May 1, 2001

Karen Beaumont, Director
Hamilton County Division of Family and Children
938 North 10th Street
Noblesville, IN 46060

Dear Ms. Beaumont:

I would like to apply for the position of Children's Services Coordinator as advertised in the April 25 issue of the *Indianapolis Star*. I believe that my qualifications and expertise would enable me to fulfill the duties and responsibilities of the position in an exemplary manner.
Enclosed please find a current résumé. I call your attention to my professional aspirations, education, and experience. I sincerely want to continue to work with at-risk children and their families. I worked for 4 years as a child welfare specialist with Family Outreach here in Indianapolis and currently work part-time as a social service assistant to the director of the Child and Family Services Center. I am completing my advanced field practicum experience at the Child and Family Services Center as well. In that role, I provide case management and supportive counseling services to children and families affected by domestic violence, substance misuse, academic problems, juvenile delinquency, and mental or physical illness and disability.

I am on course to receive the bachelor of social work degree and a certificate in case management from Indiana University in 2 weeks. I expect to graduate near the top of my class. My academic record and references support my qualifications for the advertised position. I am bilingual with excellent verbal and written communication skills in both English and Spanish. I enjoy people and possess the ability to lead or to follow as needed. I view myself as a responsible and reliable team player capable of performing effectively under pressure.

Thank you for taking the time to review this letter and my résumé. I hope you find that my qualifications and credentials match your needs. I would genuinely like to talk with you in person to discuss the position and learn more about your organization. If you have any questions or would like to arrange a meeting, please feel free to telephone me at either my home (317) 274-0001 or office (317) 274-6705.

Sincerely yours,

Maria Sanchez, B.S.W. (expected May 13, 2001)

Enc.

Appendix 7
Action Verbs for Use in Developing Learning Plans

Action verbs are used to describe a particular activity you might perform in pursuing a learning objective or demonstrating achievement. We have organized these verbs according to Bloom's Cognitive Taxonomy of Learning Objectives. You may wish to refer to the list when you are attempting to create useful learning objectives.

ACTION VERBS FOR LEARNING

Recall	Comprehension	Application	Analysis	Synthesis	Evaluation
Duplicate	Classify	Adapt	Analyze	Arrange	Appraise
Identify	Construe	Adopt	Appraise	Assemble	Arbitrate
Label	Define	Apply	Audit	Build	Argue
List	Describe	Choose	Break down	Collect	Assay
Locate	Discuss	Consume	Calculate	Combine	Assess
Match	Explain	Demonstrate	Categorize	Compile	Choose
Memorize	Express	Develop	Chart	Compose	Compare
Name	Indicate	Dramatize	Compare	Constitute	Criticize
Order	Locate	Employ	Contrast	Construct	Decree
Point out	Recognize	Exercise	Criticize	Create	Defend
Recall	Report	Exploit	Diagram	Design	Determine
Recognize	Restate	Illustrate	Differentiate	Develop	Estimate
Relate	Review	Implement	Discriminate	Effect	Evaluate
Remember	Select	Interpret	Dissect	Form	Grade
Repeat	State	Operate	Distinguish	Formulate	Judge
Reproduce	Translate	Practice	Examine	Generate	Predict
Tell		Schedule	Experiment	Manage	Rank
Underline		Sketch	Inventory	Organize	Rate
		Solve	Question	Originate	Select
		Use	Study	Plan	Support
			Test	Prepare	Value
				Propose	
				Set up	
				Write	

Appendix 8
Social Work Portfolio Documents
Checklist

Please consider the array of documents you might include in your social work portfolio. Be sure to identify other documents that you have or intend to include. Circle Y (Yes, I already have included this form of documentation), N (No, I have not included this documentation and do not plan to do so), or I (I intend to include the documentation within my portfolio) as appropriate.

Y N I   Outer Title Page (of expandable folder or large three-ring binder or first page of an electronic presentation)

Y N I   Submission Letter

Y N I   Inner Title Page (name, date, address, phone number)

Y N I   Table of Contents

Y N I   Introductory Statement

Y N I   Résumé

Y N I   Personal Statement

Y N I   Learning Products (e.g., papers, reports, essays that you have written or published)

Y N I   Self-assessment of each learning product

Y N I   Summary

Y N I   Appendix containing college or university transcripts

Y N I   Appendix containing copies of diplomas, certificates, awards, professional licenses

Y N I   Appendix containing copies of letters of reference or recommendation

Y N I   Appendix containing copies of performance evaluations or appraisals

Y N I   Appendix containing other documents (please specify)

Y N I   References and Bibliography (if applicable)

Bibliography

American Psychological Association. (1994). *Publication manual of the American Psychological Association* (4th ed.). Washington, DC: Author.

Association of Social Work Boards. (2000, July 28). *Examination content outlines.* Association of Social Work Boards. Available: www.aswb.org/licensing/content.html.

Barr, R. B., & Tagg, J. (1995). From teaching to learning: A new paradigm for undergraduate education. *Change, 27*(6), 13–25.

Bloom, B. S., & Krathwohl, D. R. (1956). *Taxonomy of educational objectives: The classification of educational goals, by a committee of college and university examiners. Handbook I: Cognitive domain.* New York: Longmans, Green.

Bosworth, K., & Hamilton, S. J. (1994). *Collaborative learning: Underlying processes and effective techniques.* San Francisco: Jossey-Bass.

Bringle, R. G., & Hatcher, J. A. (1996). Implementing service learning in higher education. *Journal of Higher Education, 67*(2), 221–239.

Bullock, K. (1999). Improving learning in year 9: Making use of personal learning plans. *Educational Studies, 25*(1), 19–34.

Bureau of Labor Statistics. (2000, August 6). *Occupational handbook.* U.S. Department of Labor Bureau of Labor Statistics. Available: www.stats.bls.gov/oco/ocos060.htm.

Challis, M. (1999). AMEE medical education guide number 11 (revised): Portfolio-based learning and assessment in medical education. *Medical Teacher, 21*(4), 370–387.

Challis, M. (2000). AMEE medical education guide number 19: Personal learning plans. *Medical Teacher, 22*(3), 225–237.

Chickering, A. W., & Gamson, Z. F. (1987). Seven principles for good practice in undergraduate education. *AAHE Bulletin, 39*(7), 3–7.

Cohen, N. H. (1995). *Mentoring adult learners: A guide for educators and trainers.* Malabar, FL: Krieger.

Commission on Accreditation of the Council on Social Work Education. (1994). *Handbook of accreditation standards and procedures.* Alexandria, VA: Author.

Cooper, J. L. (1995). Cooperative learning and critical thinking. Special Issue: Psychologists teach critical thinking. *Teaching of Psychology, 22*(1), 7–9.

Cornesky, R., & McCool, S. A. (1992). *Total quality improvement guide for institutions of higher education.* Madison, WI: Magna.

Council on Social Work Education. (1992). *Curriculum policy statement of the Council on Social Work Education.* Alexandria, VA: Author.

Council on Social Work Education. (1996). *Statistics on social work education in the United States.* Alexandria, VA: Author.

Council on Social Work Education. (2001, April 19). *Educational policy and accreditation standards: Draft two for public comment.* Alexandria, VA: Author. Available: www.cswe.org/epas.htm.

Cournoyer, B. (1999). *A study of honesty, life-long learning, and critical thinking among members of a first-year MSW social work practice class.* Indianapolis, IN: Unpublished raw data.

Cournoyer, B. (2000). *The social work skills workbook* (3rd ed.). Belmont, CA: Brooks/Cole— Wadsworth.

Davis, S., & Botkin, J. (1994, September/October). The coming of knowledge-based businesses. *Harvard Business Review, 82,* 165–170.

Deming, W. E. (1964). *Statistical adjustment of data.* New York: Dover.

Deming, W. E. (1986). *Out of the crisis.* Cambridge, MA: MIT Center for Advanced Engineering Study.

Elder, L., & Paul, R. (2000, July 18). *Universal intellectual standards*. Foundation for Critical Thinking. Available: www.criticalthinking.org/university/unistan.html.

Engel, S. M. (1990). *With good reason: An introduction to informal fallacies*. New York: St. Martin's.

Enos, S. L., & Troppe, M. L. (1996). Service learning in the curriculum. In B. J. A. Associates (Ed.), *Service-learning in higher education: Concepts and practices* (pp. 156–181). San Francisco: Jossey-Bass.

Erikson, E. H. (1964). *Childhood and society* (2nd ed.). New York: Norton.

Erikson, E. H. (1980). *Identity and the life cycle*. New York: Norton.

Evans, R. I. (1973). *Jean Piaget, the man and his ideas by Richard I. Evans* (E. Duckworth, Trans.). New York: E. P. Dutton.

Felder, R. M. (1993). Reaching the second tier: Learning and teaching styles in college science education. *Journal of College Science Teaching, 23*(5), 286–290.

Felder, R. M., & Silverman, L. K. (1988). Learning styles and teaching styles in engineering education. *Engineering Education, 78*(7), 674–681.

Felder, R. M., & Solomon, B. A. (2000, July 18). *Learning styles and strategies*. Available: www2.ncsu.edu/unity/lockers/users/f/felder/public/ILSdir/styles.htm.

Foundation for Critical Thinking. (2000, July 18). *Valuable intellectual traits*. Available: www.criticalthinking.org/university/intraits.html.

Freud, S. (1975). *Three essays on the theory of sexuality*. New York: Basic Books.

Gambrill, E. D. (1990). *Critical thinking in clinical practice: Improving the accuracy of judgments and decisions about clients*. San Francisco: Jossey-Bass.

Gambrill, E. D. (1997). *Social work practice: A critical thinker's guide*. New York: Oxford University Press.

Gardner, H. (1983). *Frames of mind: The theory of multiple intelligences*. New York: Basic Books.

Gardner, H. (1993). *Frames of mind: The theory of multiple intelligences* (2nd ed.). New York: Basic Books.

Gardner, H. (1999). *Intelligence reframed: Multiple intelligences for the 21st century*. New York: Basic Books.

Garside, C. (1996, July). Look who's talking: A comparison of lecture and group discussion teaching strategies in developing critical thinking skills. *Communication Education, 45*, 212–227.

Gibbs, L., & Gambrill, E. (1996). *Critical thinking for social workers: A workbook*. Thousand Oaks, CA: Pine Forge Press.

Gibbs, L. E. (1991). *Scientific reasoning for social workers: Bridging the gap between research and practice*. New York: Macmillan.

Gibbs, L. E. (1994). Teaching clinical reasoning. *The Behavior Therapist, 17*(1), 1–6.

Gibelman, M. (1995). *What social workers do*. Washington, DC: NASW Press.

Gibelman, M., & Schervish, P. H. (1993). *Who we are: The social work labor force as reflected in the NASW membership*. Washington, DC: NASW Press.

Gibelman, M., & Schervish, P. H. (1996). *Who we are: A second look* (2nd ed.). Washington, DC: NASW Press.

Gilligan, C. (1982). *In a different voice: Psychological theory and women's development*. Cambridge, MA: Harvard University Press.

Goleman, D. (1995). *Emotional intelligence*. New York: Bantam Books.

Goleman, D. (1998). *Working with emotional intelligence*. New York: Bantam Books.

Handy, C. (1989). *The age of unreason*. Boston: Harvard Business School Press.

Havighurst, R. J. (1953). *Developmental tasks and education* (2nd ed.). New York: David McKay.

Herrmann, N. (1990). *The creative brain*. Lake Lure, NC: Brain Books.

Hoffer, E. (1973). *Reflections on the human condition*. New York: Harper & Row.

Holland, J. L. (1985a). *Making vocational choices: A theory of vocational personalities and work environments* (2nd ed.). Englewood Cliffs, NJ: Prentice Hall.

Holland, J. L. (1985b). *The Self-Directed Search* (2nd ed.). Odessa, FL: Psychological Assessment Resources.

Holland, J. L. (1997). *Making vocational choices: A theory of vocational personalities and work environments* (3rd ed.). Odessa, FL: Psychological Assessment Resources.

Holland, J. L., Powell, A. B., & Fritzsche, B. A. (1994). *The Self-Directed Search (SDS) professional user's guide* (2nd ed.). Odessa, FL: Psychological Assessment Resources.

Hooker, M. (1997). The transformation of higher education. In D. G. Oblinger & S. C. Rush (Eds.), *The learning revolution: The challenge of information technology in the academy* (pp. 20–34). Bolton, MA: Anker.

Hubbard, D. L. (Ed.). (1993). *Continuous quality improvement: Making the transition to education*. Maryville, MO: Prescott.

Huff, M. T., & Johnson, M. M. (1998). Empowering students in a graduate level social work course. *Journal of Social Work Education, 34*(3), 375–385.

Johnstone, S. M., & Krauth, B. (1996). Balancing quality and access: Some principles of good practice for the virtual university. *Change, 28*(2), 38–41.

Joint Initiative of Mental Health Professional Organizations. (2000, July 14). *Mental health bill of rights project: Principles for the provision of mental health and substance abuse treatment services*. Available: www.socialworkers.org/practice/mental.htm.

Kaplan, R. M. (1994). *Sure-hire cover letters*. New York: AMACOM.

Keirsey, D. (1998). *Please understand me II: Temperament, character, intelligence*. Del Mar, CA: Prometheus Nemesis.

Keirsey, D., & Bates, M. (1984). *Please understand me: Character and temperament types*. (4th ed.). Del Mar, CA:: Prometheus Nemesis.

Knowles, M. (1980). *Modern practice of adult education*. Chicago: Follett.

Knowles, M. (1990). *The adult learner: A neglected species*. (4th ed.). Houston: Gulf.

Knowles, M. S. (1984). *Andragogy in action: Applying modern principles of adult learning*. San Francisco: Jossey-Bass.

Knowles, M. S. (1989). Everything you wanted to know from Malcolm Knowles (and weren't afraid to ask). *Training, 26*(8), 45–50.

Knowles, M. S. (1992). Applying principles of adult learning in conference presentations. *Adult Learning, 4*(1), 11–14.

Knowles, M. S., Holton, E. F., III, & Swanson, R. A. (1998). *The adult learner* (5th ed.). Houston, TX: Gulf.

Kohlberg, L., Levine, C., & Hewer, A. (1983). *Moral stages: A current formulation and a response to critics*. New York: Karger.

Kolb, D. A. (1984). *Experiential learning: Experience as the source of learning and development*. Englewood Cliffs, NJ: Prentice Hall.

Kolb, D. A. (1999). *Learning Style Inventory: Version 3*. Boston: Hay/McBer.

Kolb, D. A., Osland, J. S., & Rubin, I. M. (Eds.). (1994). *The organizational behavior reader*. Englewood Cliffs, NJ: Prentice Hall.

Kolb, D. A., Rubin, I. M., & Osland, J. S. (1994). *Organizational behavior: An experiential approach*. Englewood Cliffs, NJ: Prentice Hall.

Krathwohl, D. R., Bloom, B. S., & Masia, B. B. (1964). *Taxonomy of educational objectives: The classification of educational goals. Handbook II: Affective domain*. New York: David McKay.

Lawrence, G. (1994). *People types and tiger stripes* (3rd ed.). Gainesville, FL: Center for Applications of Psychological Type.

Leavitt, M. O. (1997). A learning enterprise for the cybercentury: The Western Governors University. In D. G. Oblinger & S. C. Rush (Eds.), *The learning revolution: The challenge of information technology in the academy* (pp. 20–34). Bolton, MA: Anker.

Lewis, R. G., & Smith, D. H. (1994). *Total quality in higher education*. Delray Beach, FL: St. Lucie Press.

Lohman, D. F. (1989). Human intelligence: An introduction to advances in theory and research. *Review of Educational Research, 59*(4), 333–373.

Maslow, A. H. (1968). *Toward a psychology of being* (2nd Rev. ed.). New York: Reinhold.

Mayer, J. D., & Salovey, P. (1997). What is emotional intelligence? In P. Salovey & D. Sluyter (Eds.), *Emotional development and emotional intelligence: Implications for educators* (pp. 3–31). New York: Basic Books.

McBurney, D.H. (1995). The problem method of teaching research methods. Special Issue: Psychologists teach critical thinking. *Teaching of Psychology, 22*(1), 36–38.

Moore, B. N., & Parker, R. (1995). *Critical thinking* (4th ed.). Mountain View, CA: Mayfield.

Morgan, R. B., & Smith, J. E. (1996). *Staffing the new workplace: Selecting and promoting for quality improvement*. Milwaukee, WI: ASQC Quality Press.

Myers, I. (1962). *Manual: The Myers-Briggs Type Indicator*. Palo Alto, CA: Consulting Psychologists Press.

National Association of Social Workers. (1973). *Standards for social service manpower*. Washington, DC: Author.

National Association of Social Workers. (1981). *Standards for the classification of social work practice*. Silver Spring, MD: Author.

National Association of Social Workers. (1999). *Code of ethics of the National Association of Social Workers*. Washington, DC: Author.

Oblinger, D. G., & Rush, S. C. (1997). The learning revolution. In D. G. Oblinger & S. C. Rush (Eds.), *The learning revolution: The challenge of information technology in the academy* (pp. 1–19). Bolton, MA: Anker.

Paul, R. (1993). *Critical thinking: What every person needs to survive in a rapidly changing world* (Rev. 3rd ed.). Santa Rosa, CA: Foundation for Critical Thinking.

Perry, W. G. (1970). *Forms of intellectual and ethical development in the college years.* New York: Holt, Rinehart & Winston.

Phillips, C., Prue, J. F., Hasazi, S. B., & Morgan, P. (2000). Personal learning plans: Building collaboration among teachers, students with disabilities, and their parents. *NASSP Bulletin, 84*(6), 13–28.

Putnam, J. W. (1997). *Cooperative learning in diverse classrooms.* Upper Saddle River, NJ: Merrill.

Roberts, H. V. (Ed.). (1995). *Academic initiatives in total quality for higher education.* Milwaukee, WI: ASQC Quality Press.

Salovey, P., & Mayer, J. D. (1990). Emotional intelligence. *Imagination, Cognition and Personality, 9*(3), 185–211.

Senge, P. M. (1990). *The fifth discipline: The art and practice of the learning organization.* New York: Doubleday/Currency.

Senge, P. M. (1992). Building learning organizations. *Journal of Quality and Participation, 15*(2), 30–38.

Senge, P. M., Kleiner, A., Roberts, C., Ross, R. B., & Smith, B. J. (1994). *The fifth discipline fieldbook: Strategies and tools for building a learning organization.* New York: Doubleday/Currency.

Sherr, L. A., & Teeter, D. J. (Eds.). (1991). *Total quality management in higher education.* San Francisco: Jossey-Bass.

Silvestri, G. T. (1997, November). Occupation employment projections to 2006. *Monthly Labor Review,* 58–83.

Solomon, B. A., & Felder, R. M. (2000, July 10). *Index of Learning Styles.* Available: www.crc4mse.org/ILS/Index.html.

Super, D. E., & Jordaan, J. P. (1973). Career development theory. *British Journal of Guidance and Counseling, 1,* 3–16.

Sutherland, T. E., & Bonwell, C. C. (Eds.). (1996). *Using active learning in college classes: A range of options for faculty.* San Francisco: Jossey-Bass.

Tieger, P. D., & Barron-Tieger, B. (1992). *Do what you are: Discover the perfect career for you through the secrets of psychological type.* Boston: Little, Brown.

Toffler, A. (1983). *The third wave.* New York: Bantam Books.

Toffler, A., & Toffler, H. (1995). *Creating a new civilization: The politics of the third wave.* Atlanta, GA: Turner.

Wilcox, S. (1996). Fostering self-directed learning in the university setting. *Studies in Higher Education, 21*(2), 165–177.

Index